Shepherd of Souls
RECOVERING *the* LOST ART
of the PASTORAL

BENJAMIN ISRAEL ROBINSON
ONEING PUBLICATIONS

Copyright © 2016 by Benjamin Israel Robinson
All rights reserved. No part of this book may be reproduced,
scanned, or distributed in any printed or
electronic form without permission.
First Edition: May 2016
Printed in the United States of America
ISBN: 978-0-692-71995-4

For the Bride;
may true shepherds arise within you to wash you with water by the
word, clothe you in white garments, and prepare you
for the marriage supper of the Lamb.

Contents

Acknowledgements

There is no way I would have completed this book without the support, encouragement, and instruction of a throng of individuals too great to number in this space. However, I cannot go on without at least mentioning a few of the people who have carried me thus far.

Many thanks to my wonderfully supportive wife, Sunhee. You have made great sacrifices to make room for me to continue to write, to create, and to explore the many inspirations that continually prod my heart. You have no idea how much your love means to me, and how strong you make me!

And to my parents, Bishops Peter and Diane Robinson—my first and most significant rabbis. You taught me to love the Lord, to study his Word, to seek his face, and to follow his plan for my life above all things. I am who I am because I've watched the way you live your lives and I've emulated the example that you've set for me!

To Bishop Robert Daniels, my spiritual father: this book is in large part the fruit of your patient instruction in my life. The aroma of your wisdom emerges from every page of this book.

To Archbishop Kirby Clements: you have no idea what an inspiration and an encouragement you are to me. The fact that you take the time both to encourage my writing and to prophesy to me about what God will do through my books is like wind beneath my wings. I owe you a great debt.

To Pastor Mike Perkinson: I've recently been reminded of the good deposit that God has entrusted to my care through your teaching. God has used you to build a foundation in me that supports me in all that I do. The writing of this book was no exception.

Special thanks also to Phillip Lee and Christa Cho for their early labors in the editorial process, and to Marisa Thompson for her tenacious work on the final edit of the manuscript.

Finally, I give all of the praise, glory, and honor to the God and Father of our Lord Jesus Christ, the Father of mercies, to Jesus the Good Shepherd and the Overseer of our souls, and to the Spirit of Holiness who indwells our hearts and brings us into the new creation.

Preface

*The members of my first congregation
were blades of grass.*

When I was in the ninth grade, I worked as the assistant janitor on my high school campus. Every day after all of the other students went home, I went about the school emptying garbage cans, sweeping up tanbark, and watering all of the lawns and flower beds on the campus. And as I worked, I preached . . . I preached the gospel to the tanbark and to the grass and to the flowers. It was a wonderfully formative time in the development of both my walk with God and my sense of calling to the ministry.

I knew that I wanted to be a minister of the gospel from the time I was very young, but I also knew that I needed to know what God had called me to do with my life, so I began seeking direction from him at a young age. God answered my prayers by calling me into his service when I was eleven years old. He spoke clearly to my heart and told me that he would send me to the ends of the earth as a proclaimer of the gospel.

These formative years of my life corresponded to David's years as a shepherd over the flock of his father, Jesse. Those years were hard years—years in which I felt isolated and alone.

Yet I was keenly aware of the fact that the Lord had set me apart and drawn me to himself.

I spent a lot of time dreaming during those years . . . dreaming of being a shepherd in the house of God, of leading his people to streams of living water, and of being a steward of the Word and the Spirit. But the task of preaching the gospel was at the heart of all of my hopes and dreams for ministry. I knew that I was called of God to be a shepherd in his house, but what I didn't know was that the task of preaching the gospel was only a small part of that–in fact, a minuscule part of the overall task of shepherding the flock of God. I would discover this in a dramatic way once I planted our church, Living Hope, with my wife in January of 2004.

The first years of our pastoral ministry at Living Hope were experimental years as we sought to discover our particular method for making disciples of Jesus Christ. The preaching was powerful and effective, but most of our people needed more— they needed help understanding, appropriating, and applying the content of what was preached to their everyday lives. They needed help with their marriages, their jobs, their emotions, their habits and behaviors, and we worked frantically to try to discern the precise nature of their needs and deliver the solutions they longed for.

But in our zeal, we found ourselves working in ways that didn't correspond with the particular gifts God had given us. We found ourselves trying to be therapists, marriage counselors, and life coaches. We would sit with people for hours over a period of weeks and months and see little to no changes in their lives. Quite often the people whom we spent the most time with and gave the most attention to walked away from us in a flurry of offense, leaving us baffled and confused, wondering what in the world had happened.

Slowly we began to discover that there is no standard definition of the work of a shepherd–that no two shepherds look exactly the same. I had spent so much time feeling guilty about what I couldn't do that I hadn't seen the beauty of what I could do. But as I began to discover the limits of the gifts God had given me, I began to make some changes in the way I undertook the pastoral task.

What I discovered is that the true ministry of the pastor is not about preaching, teaching, or dynamic and visionary leadership. The true nature of the pastoral task is the act of coming alongside individuals and leading them into an ever-deepening walk with Christ by the power of the Holy Spirit. As I realized this, I began to discover that God had placed many members in my congregation who were far more gifted in the task of shepherding than I was, and I began to see that my true gift was to identify these people and empower them to exercise their gifts with greater confidence and competence.

Inspired by this revelation, I created a course called *Shepherd of Souls* and I aimed it at a group of members of our church who never would have seen themselves as having a pastoral gift. The main teaching of the course was that the true task of the pastor is not to be an administrator of programs but a shepherd of souls. The spiritual leader is one who knows how to shepherd the soul: how to deal with negative thought patterns in a way that renews the mind, how to manage destructive emotions in a way that encourages the heart, and how to soften the stubbornness of the will so it may be brought into alignment with God's desires. All of our pastoral activities are nothing more than attempts to bring the mind, the will, and the emotions into alignment with God's Word and into fellowship with God's Spirit.

Over the past eight years, I have taught this course multiple times and have continued to develop its content. This book is a product of that labor. In the following pages I will attempt to elucidate the true nature of the task of shepherding the soul by drawing insights from Scripture, Christian theology, and personal experience. My prayer is that God will use these pages to increase your confidence in your ability (by God's power) to shepherd the souls of those entrusted to your care.

Sincerely,
Benjamin Israel Robinson
May 2016

Introduction

My soul follows hard after you.

(Psalm 63:8)

These words of the psalmist communicate the ideal state of the Christian soul: being led by the Spirit at all times, living in the continual awareness of God's presence, power, and love, and in joyful obedience to his Word. The realization of this state is the goal of all of our spiritual activities: worship, prayer, study of Scripture, fellowship, teaching, serving, etc. All that comprises the Christian life has this ideal state of being as its objective.

But for most of us, remaining in this state feels impossible. Our souls are often like sheep that wander off and are led astray, and when this happens we find ourselves venturing into the realm that the Bible refers to as *the flesh* instead of remaining in the flow of the Spirit's life.

However, our souls don't wander off without good reason. If you are a believer in Jesus Christ, you have a natural desire to remain in him, to live in him, and to find your being in him. So why is it so hard to live out this desire? What is it that entices you and convinces you to depart from the presence of the Lord, like Cain, in order to live in the land of Nod (*nod* means *wandering* in Hebrew)?

The answer to that question is simple: pain. The soul

experiences pain when it is deprived of something that it deems indispensable. Rejection, criticism, abandonment, failure, deprivation . . . all of these experiences (and more) are intensely painful for the soul, and they strip the soul of its sense of well-being and peace.

REPENTANCE & REST

The Bible speaks of this deprived state as the affliction of the soul; the soul is afflicted when it is deprived of anything it deems necessary. That being the case, it seems strange to discover that God commanded his people to participate in practices that would purposefully afflict the soul. The primary example from the Old Testament which comes to mind at this point is Sabbath observance. The book of Leviticus describes the experience of the Sabbath in these words: *It shall be a Sabbath of rest unto you, and you shall afflict your souls* (Leviticus 16:31). First God says the Sabbath is about rest, and then he says it is an affliction of the soul. How can it be restful and afflictive at the same time?

Rest (especially Sabbath rest) requires the repression of the urge to *do*. The soul seeks satisfaction in the works of the body; the Sabbath deprives the soul of the fruit of this quest by forcing it to stop. By and large, rest is not something we sign up for; God has to *make* us lie down in green pastures, and this can be painfully afflictive to the soul.

This is what the Sovereign Lord, the Holy One of Israel, says: "In repentance and rest is your salvation, in quietness and trust is your strength," but you would have none of it. (Isaiah 30:15)

How often has God offered us salvation and strength, but we would have none of it because we didn't want repentance, rest, quietness, or trust–we wanted labor, pleasure, success, indulgence . . . ?

Repentance is here associated with rest. To repent means to change your mind, to change what you think. You don't have access to what you really think, to what you really believe, until you find yourself in the throes of temptation. Temptation reveals your true belief system. James says that we are tempted when we are led astray by our own evil desires and enticed (James 1:14).

At the moment of temptation you have access to your true thoughts, to your true beliefs . . . and it is therefore only at the moment of temptation that true repentance can take place. You can't change what you think if you don't know what you really think. Temptation is another way in which the soul is afflicted. God allows us to experience temptation, not to lead us into it, but to deliver us out of it. He allows us to experience it in order to grant us the gift of repentance.

God must grant you repentance (2 Timothy 2:25), and he is able to do so only in the midst of your moment of temptation. God offers you the gift of repentance precisely at the place in which your soul is afflicted. And when God grants you repentance in the moment of your affliction, you discover that your soul was afflicted because you were thinking wrongly about your situation and were unaware of how accessible God's presence, power, and love were to you at that very moment.

I experienced this recently on the eighth day of a ten-day fast. It was evening time and I had hit a wall, and I felt that I just couldn't make it another day. So I told my wife that I was leaving. When she asked where I was going, I told her that I was going out to eat dinner by myself. "But aren't you fasting two more days?" she asked. At this point I informed her that I had fasted long enough and was ending it early. She smiled and said, "Okay, that's fine; end your fast early if you want, but not tonight. Go into your office and just pray tonight, and tomorrow morning if you still want to end your fast, eat whatever you want." I didn't like this proposition because I was inflamed with desire to gorge on the biggest burrito I could possibly find, but my wife spoke with a spirit of wisdom that I couldn't resist, so I reluctantly retreated to my office to pretend to pray.

The moment the door to my office closed behind me I felt the immediate temptation to put on my earphones, turn on Netflix, and veg the night away. However, I knew that my wife had made a sacrifice by giving me the evening to pray, seeing that she would have to handle the full responsibility of getting our daughter ready for bed and putting her down to sleep. So I got on my knees and tried to pray, but I just couldn't connect. There was no wind, no earthquake, no fire . . . and no still small voice either. I felt completely disconnected from God and wholly devoid of any desire to reconnect with him.

I left off trying to pray and began to meditate on Psalm 23:1: *The Lord is my shepherd, I shall not want.* I repeated the verse in my mind over and over and over again. I focused all of my attention on each word of this verse and resolved to rest there until the Spirit of God caused my heart to awaken to his presence. Within twenty minutes or so my spirit began to come alive and the presence of the Lord began to draw near. Suddenly my mind became sensitive to his truth and my heart began to respond to his love. I spent the entire evening there, seeking the face of God and listening to his voice. The wind began to blow, the earth began to shake, the fire began to burn, and the voice of God began to speak to me.

At some point during the course of the evening I forgot that I was hungry, and by the end of the night I felt so fully satisfied in the presence of the Lord that I felt as if I never needed to eat again. And just after midnight I came out of my office, found my wife, and said to her, "I can't believe I almost traded this in for a burrito!"

Not only did I finish my ten days of fasting, but I went on fasting for a few more days—not because I felt obligated to, but because I simply didn't feel like I needed to eat. Looking back on the experience, I realized I had come to a richly satisfying place in God in the midst of one of the most intense times of restless dissatisfaction in my life.

THE SOUL'S SATISFACTION

The affliction of the soul is a gift from God, because God can only satisfy the soul in the moment of its affliction. God cannot grant rest to the indulgent soul; it must be afflicted and deprived. We must come to our moment of affliction before we can find the Lord to be our shepherd. Moses alludes to this truth in describing the forty years of wandering in the wilderness by the people of God:

> *Remember how the Lord led you all the way through the wilderness these forty years, to humble and to test you, in order to know what was in your heart, whether or not you would keep his commands. He humbled you, causing you to hunger, then feeding you with manna, which neither you nor your fathers had known, to teach you that man does not live by bread alone, but by every word that proceeds from the mouth of God. Your clothes did not wear out and your feet did not swell during these forty years. Know then in your heart that as a man disciplines his son, so the Lord your God disciplines you.* (Deuteronomy 8:2–5)

Did you see that? *To humble and to test you* . . . he led you through the wilderness in order to humble you and to test you. He humbled you by causing you to hunger . . . then he tested you to see what you would do in the throes of hunger . . . and then he fed you with manna. The whole experience was designed to bring out what was in the heart.

God is greater than my hunger, but he must allow me to

hunger in order to teach me that he is greater than my hunger. The revelation that God is greater than my hunger is only made available to me in the midst of the experience of hunger. Remember the temptation of Jesus? The tempter didn't come to him until he got hungry!

Abstinence afflicts the soul, and the afflicted soul cannot find its own way: it needs a shepherd to lead it into the place of satisfaction. Pain disconnects the soul from its experiential connection to the Spirit of God. When the soul is in pain, it feels disconnected from the life of God and naturally begins to fear that it has been forsaken and abandoned. This is why you can come right out of a powerful time of prayer and get in a big fight with your spouse, or lose your cool when someone cuts you off on the freeway. When the soul experiences pain, it feels lost, left to itself, and abandoned.

It is at this very place that the soul needs a shepherd. The soul cannot lead itself back into the experiential awareness of God's presence and love; it must be led. And it is this very place at which we may come to know Jesus as the Shepherd and Overseer of our souls–if we choose him as our shepherd (1 Peter 2:25). We have options: another shepherd also presents itself to the soul in its moment of agony. That shepherd is what the Bible calls *the flesh*.

The flesh is actually nothing more than the abandonment of ourselves to ourselves. We are in the flesh when we determine to make a way for ourselves, declaring our independence from

God. Here we cease to wait upon the Lord and begin to take matters into our own hands. This is why Paul differentiates between the fruit of the Spirit (Galatians 5:22) and the works of the flesh (Galatians 5:19-21). When we are walking in the Spirit, we must wait for the Spirit to make us fruitful. But when we are walking in the flesh, we must work to make provision for our own needs and desires. The flesh works; the Spirit bears fruit.

When it is in the flesh, the soul does not follow hard after God, but after itself. This self-shepherding takes the forms of self-preservation, self-gratification, and self-actualization. The soul preserves itself through anger and its machinations, all of which are designed to deter the possibility of further loss. The soul gratifies itself through lust and its machinations, all of which are designed to procure ever-increasing levels of satisfaction and delight. And the soul actualizes itself through labor and its machinations, all of which are designed to enable the soul to find fulfillment in the manifestation of its own gifts and abilities.

When the soul is afflicted, it must either throw itself upon God, or it will indulge itself. The soul justifies its decision to indulge itself by believing that it has been wrongly deprived and that it deserves to be satisfied. This is how a man who lacks food to eat can make himself feel okay about stealing someone else's food or money and a man whose wife deprives him sexually can make himself feel okay about satisfying his desires outside the marriage covenant.

In the hour of temptation, the carnal mind seeks to find a justification for the sin which the soul desires to commit. The soul hesitates at the door of sin because it has the knowledge of good and evil. But it does not depart from evil immediately because its desire for sin increases the longer it lingers in the flesh. The soul lingers to give the mind the time it needs to find a rationalization. *I'll only do it this once more. It's really not that big of a deal. I've had a really tough day. I need something to help me make it . . .*

But the witness of Scripture is clear: the flesh profits nothing (John 6:63). Ultimately, when left to their own devices, our souls are utterly incapable of preserving themselves, gratifying themselves, or actualizing themselves. And those who live according to the flesh inevitably find themselves longing to fill their stomachs with the pods that the pigs are eating. However, it is then, when we recognize the bankruptcy of life in the flesh, that our souls become ready to pass under the staff of the true Shepherd and Overseer of our souls.

THE PASTORAL TASK

While Jesus is the ultimate Shepherd and Overseer of every soul who believes in him, he has also extended an invitation for us to participate in this glorious pastoral task. Understanding the nature and significance of this pastoral task is essential for the recovery of a truly biblical definition of leadership in the body of Christ.

Hebrews 13:17 admonishes us to obey our leaders and submit to their authority because they watch over our souls. The definition of leadership presented in this passage is foreign to that which is popular in our culture. In our culture, leadership is about being responsible for a set of tasks and about being capable of inspiring a group of people to complete those tasks. But in the New Testament, leadership is not about the execution of a task, but about of the stewardship of souls.

The leader is one who watches over souls, and this language of 'watching over' is pastoral language. Shepherds watched over their flocks by night in biblical times. When the Scripture says that leaders are those who watch over souls, it means that the job of the spiritual leader is to be a shepherd of souls. Leadership in the body of Christ is pastoral in nature, not administrative. The true work of the leader in the New Testament church is to bring people progressively closer to a life lived in the continual awareness of the presence and power of God, saturated in his holy Word, and overflowing with his holy love.

However, to say that leadership in the body of Christ is inherently pastoral is not to say that all Christian leaders are pastors. All Christian leadership is pastoral, but not all Christian leaders are pastors. There is a difference between the pastoral and the pastor.

In Ephesians 4, Paul enumerates five offices of ministry which comprise the government of the body of Christ: apostles, prophets, evangelists, pastors, and teachers. Each of these offices corresponds to a set of functions to which all believers have access, but which are simply manifested in a higher measure by those who have been appointed to these offices by the Lord.

The teacher is one who has a unique gift of instruction for the body of Christ. However, all Christians can teach to some degree. If you know something about the content of the book of John that your friend doesn't know, and your friend asks you a question about the content of the book of John, you will have an opportunity to instruct your friend about the gospel of John. This doesn't necessarily mean that you are a teacher in the sense Paul uses. It simply means you tapped into a teaching moment that the Spirit of God set up for you.

Likewise, it is clear that all believers can share the gospel with those who do not know Christ, even though all believers are not evangelists. This means that all believers can be evangelistic without being evangelists. The same can be said of the prophetic and the apostolic offices.

From this it follows that the pastor is one who has a unique gift for shepherding souls in a way that leads people into a deeper daily walk with Christ. However, all Christians can shepherd souls as the Spirit leads. If your sister in Christ gets slain in the flesh[1] and can't seem to pull herself out, you have an opportunity to shepherd her soul out of the flesh and back into the realm of the Spirit. But taking this opportunity doesn't make you a pastor—it simply means that you can tap into a pastoral moment that the Spirit sets up for you.

All believers are potentially pastoral even though only a few believers are actual pastors. However, few believers ever find themselves operating in the pastoral gifts because they don't realize that they have access to them, and that the body of Christ desperately needs all believers to learn how to use the gifts. We have relegated the pastoral to the office of the pastor instead of using the office of the pastor to show the whole body how to function pastorally, and in doing so we demonstrate that we don't really understand the purpose of the offices of ministry to begin with.

Paul reveals the purposes of the fivefold ministry gifts as edification and empowerment: the gifts are designed by Christ to build up the body and to equip its members for the work of ministry (Ephesians 4:11ff). But what is the work of ministry? Each gift should reproduce the type of ministry corresponding to its own kind. Pastors should empower people to operate in the pastoral, just as evangelists should empower people to evangelize and prophets should empower people to prophesy.

This book is about the pastoral task, but it is not just a book for pastors. My fundamental proposal is that the pastoral task is not accomplished solely by the pastors in the body of Christ. The pastoral task is rightly undertaken by the whole body of Christ. We are called to be a shepherding people, not just a shepherded people. This book is offered as an attempt to present a biblical model of what that means and to show how we can take steps to live out this vision with power.

1

God's Preference for the Shepherd

And the Lord respected Abel and his offering, but he did not respect Cain and his offering.

(Genesis 4:4-5)

The term *pastor* was coined in the mid 13th century from the French *pasteur* and the Latin *pastorum,* both meaning *shepherd* or *herdsman.* It has the same root as the term *pasture,* and it follows that the task of the spiritual shepherd is to lead a flock of sheep to green pastures where they may graze safely. The most common Hebrew term translated *shepherd* in the Old Testament is *raha,* and it appears some 144 times. The prevalence of this term throughout the Old Testament indicates the importance of the concept of the shepherd in Israel's life and history.

The first occurrence of the term is found in Genesis 4, in

which Cain and Abel bring offerings to God from their respective fields of work. God looks with favor upon the offering of Abel and rejects the offering of Cain. The fact that the Bible doesn't tell us why God rejects Cain's offering is troubling to the modern mind. The only distinction between them mentioned in the passage is that Abel was a keeper of sheep and Cain worked the soil: God rejected the offering of the farmer and accepted the offering of the shepherd.

While the reason for this scandal of particularity is not found within the story itself, I believe we can discover the reason by considering what is *behind* the story. In order to take a peek behind the story, we must consider its historical setting.

THE WILDERNESS COMMUNITY

While Mosaic authorship of the Pentateuch is an idea that very few contemporary biblical scholars espouse,[2] I would argue that seeing the wilderness of Sinai as the birthplace of the creation narrative of Genesis provides us with a crystal clear picture of what was going on in this particular story, and it also helps us understand why the role of the shepherd was so important within the history of Israel.

Even if Moses did not pen every word of the Pentateuch himself, the story is *Mosaic* in that its origins are to be found within the years of wandering in the wilderness. It was there that Moses received, by divine revelation, the account of the creation of the world that we have in the opening chapters of our Bible.[3]

And it was there that Moses delivered this story to a community of wanderers 400 years removed from their historic roots in the land of the patriarchs.

The critical thing to understand about the patriarchs is that they were a family of shepherds. Abraham was a shepherd, as were Isaac and Jacob and all of Jacob's sons. Shepherding was not just their occupation, but was at the center of their way of life. And this way of life was undisturbed for generations until a famine facilitated a confrontation between Joseph and his brothers in the land to which they had sold him as a slave.

In the aftermath of the drama of reconciliation between the sons of Jacob, the whole family relocated to Egypt where Joseph provided for them out of the abundance of his household. But all of Joseph's wealth and prestige in the land of Egypt could not overcome the reproach of their pastoral lifestyle. We see this clearly in the way Joseph prepped his family for their meeting with Pharaoh:

Then Joseph said to his brothers and to his father's household, "I will go up and tell Pharaoh, and say to him, 'My brothers and those of my father's house, who were in the land of Canaan, have come to me. And the men are shepherds, for their occupation has been to feed livestock; and they have brought their flocks, their herds, and all that they have.' So it shall be, when Pharaoh calls you and says, 'What is your occupation?' that you shall say, 'Your servants' occupation has been with livestock from our youth even till now, both we and also our fathers,' that you may *dwell in the land of Goshen; **for every shepherd is an abomination to the Egyptians.*** " (Genesis 46:31-34; emphasis mine)

Joseph instructs his brothers to ask Pharaoh to allow them to reside in the land of Goshen because Goshen was far removed from the heart of Egyptian society, and Joseph sought to protect his family from the reproach and rejection they would incur because of their pastoral vocation by giving them the space to continue practicing their craft freely.

After the death of Joseph, however, a Pharaoh arose who had no regard for him and who enslaved the people of Israel for generations. During this period of time, the people of Israel must have developed an inferiority complex regarding both their pastoral lifestyle and the history of their God. Of course, the Exodus would be a powerful step towards changing all of that, but the Exodus itself could only do so much to disrupt thought patterns which had been ingrained for generations.

But from the victorious side of the Red Sea, as the bodies of the Egyptians began to wash up on the shore, the newly-freed sons of Israel received a fresh revelation of the power of their God. This new revelation inspired a spontaneous eruption of worship, singing, and dancing as they triumphantly declared,

Who is like you, O Lord, among the gods?
Who is like you, glorious in holiness,
Fearful in praises, doing wonders? (Exodus 15:11)

It is to this community of wanderers that the story found in the Pentateuch is told. It was during these forty years of wandering that the inspiration of the Holy Spirit moved the heart of Moses to write the words we find in the Genesis narrative. The function of these books was to reconnect the people of Israel to the God of their history, the God of their fathers, and to break the sense of inferiority that had plagued their minds and hearts for generations as the result of the oppression to which they had been subjected.

To this community of wanderers in the wilderness, newly reacquainted with the God of Abraham, Isaac, and Jacob, the story of Cain and Abel would not only have made perfect sense, but would have been incredibly encouraging. From the outset of the narrative, God reveals himself through Moses to his wandering people as the God of the shepherd people. Why does God reject the offering of Cain and accept the offering of Abel? Because his preference is for the shepherd, and it is the offering of the shepherd that pleases him.

God rejects the agrarian offering of Cain (which represented Egypt's agrarian way of life) and accepts the pastoral offering of Abel (which represented the pastoral way of life handed down from Abraham, Isaac, and Jacob). The God of Israel is the God of the shepherd; his preference is for the shepherd and his covenant is with the shepherd people.

THE PREPARATION OF MOSES

This perspective also helps us understand why Moses needed to spend forty years in the wilderness of Sinai before becoming the great deliverer of Israel. When he was forty years old, Moses thought he was ready to be the deliverer and gave it his best shot. First, he killed an Egyptian, and then he tried to intervene in a conflict between two Israelites. And that was the extent of his deliverance ministry; it all came crashing down after that, and he had to run for his life into the wilderness of Midian or face the wrath of Pharaoh.

Moses had been schooled in all of the wisdom of the Egyptians (Acts 7:22). He knew their economic policy, their military strategy, their governmental structure, and everything else that pertained to the Egyptian way of life. If there was anyone who was qualified to take on the Egyptians and defeat them on behalf of Israel, it was Moses, and if there was anyone who was qualified to lead this fledgling nation into its destiny, it was Moses. But God didn't share Moses' perspective and thus allowed Moses' deliverance experiment to utterly fail right at its beginning.

In the wilderness, Moses found a family . . . something that he was never truly a part of back in Egypt, where he was always too Egyptian to be an Israelite and too much of an Israelite to be an Egyptian. Now suddenly Moses was a husband and a son and a brother and an uncle and a father. This web of relational connections was essential to his preparation for the ministry of deliverance, for God couldn't allow a man who knew nothing of family and healthy relationships to become the governor over his people. Such a man would surely prove to be a detriment to the life of Israel.

Not only was Moses given a family in the wilderness, he was given a task as well—and we can be sure that having been influenced by Egyptian society as he was, he would not have liked the job his father-in-law gave him one bit! He certainly would have preferred a task that gave him the opportunity to use his vast skill-set—perhaps he could have managed the family investments, or become the general manager over the family business, or represented the family in various negotiations. But no, the task his father-in-law gave him was to watch over the flocks and herds as the family shepherd.

This must have seemed to be a brainless task to Moses and he must have thought at that moment that no job could be further from the task he believed himself to be destined for, but he could not have been more wrong. Moses could not see it at the time, but those forty years of shepherding were his real preparation for the task of bringing deliverance to Israel. For it was there in the wilderness that God reconnected him to his pastoral history . . . the history of Abraham, Isaac, and Jacob.

Had he never become a shepherd, Moses would have led Israel into a future devoid of the pastoral lifestyle of the fathers and Israel would have looked back upon the patriarchs as followers of a way of life that had long become obsolete. Moses would have modernized Israel, and in disconnecting Israel from its historic lifestyle, Moses would have disrupted the progression of divine revelation that would lead toward Jesus of Nazareth, who declared himself to be the Good Shepherd who laid down his life for the sheep (John 10:11).

God had indeed called Moses to become the deliverer of Israel, but what Moses could not see was that in order to become the deliverer, he first had to become a shepherd. It is only from within the school of the shepherd that God selects those who will bring deliverance to his people in the course of salvation history. This truth is especially important in our day and age in which we are experiencing an explosion of desire for powerful ministry amongst the laity and a corresponding repulsion for pastoral ministry at the same time.

Invite the members of your church to a prophetic training seminar and the room will be packed out; invite them to a pastoral training seminar and you'll be able to throw a rock into the midst of the room without hitting anyone. Tell the people you're going to train them to pray for the sick and they'll get excited; tell them you're going to train them to shepherd souls and they'll tell you they're not ready. Everyone wants to minister powerfully, but no one wants to shepherd souls. Everyone wants to be a deliverer these days, but no one wants to be a shepherd!

But God is not looking for deliverers; he's looking for shepherds. Deliverers can break us out of things, but it takes a shepherd to lead us into something. God is not simply interested in finding people who are willing to break us out—in fact, God will only empower you to be a deliverer if he sees a willingness in your heart to be a shepherd! And this distinction between the deliverer and the shepherd also explains the rejection of Saul and the ascension of David to the throne of Israel.

THE ASCENSION OF THE SHEPHERD BOY

Saul had the heart of a deliverer, but he lacked the shepherd's heart. When God rejected Saul, he informed Samuel that he had found a man after his own heart who would shepherd his people Israel (1 Samuel 13:14; 2 Samuel 5:2). And where did God find this man? He found him out in a field watching over the flocks of his father, Jesse. It was out there in the fields that God began to visit David in order to demonstrate the power of the heart of the shepherd.

When a lion or bear came to destroy David's flock, the Spirit of the Lord would come upon David suddenly, and he would rise up and destroy the attacker. There in the wilderness, David learned how to watch and worship: he would watch over his flock, defending them when necessary, and he would worship the God of his fathers, playing skillfully on his harp.

No one knew then that God was preparing this young shepherd to be a great king. His father didn't know it, his brothers didn't know it, the people of his town didn't know it, and even David didn't know it. The unveiling of God's plan for

David's life began to unfold on the day the Lord commanded Samuel to go to the house of Jesse in Bethlehem and anoint one of his sons to be king of Israel.

The prophet Samuel came to Jesse's house in search of the one whom God had chosen to replace Saul as king of Israel. Jesse was elated and paraded all of his older sons before the prophet, dressed in the finest of ancient apparel. But one by one, God rejected each of them, leaving the prophet a bit frustrated. Finally, Samuel asked, "Are these all the sons you have?" Jesse replied, "There is still the youngest, but he is with the sheep" (1 Samuel 16:11). It is clear from Jesse's response that he did not consider David to be royal material. Nevertheless, Samuel insisted on seeing him, so Jesse sent for him and brought him before Samuel.

> *Now he was ruddy, with bright eyes, and good-looking. And the Lord said, "Arise, anoint him; for this is the one!" Then Samuel took the horn of oil and anointed him in the midst of his brothers; and the Spirit of the Lord came upon David from that day forward.* (1 Samuel 16:12-13)

David's family saw him as being fit for nothing greater than shepherding a flock of sheep, but God had determined to make him the shepherd of his people, Israel. David's shepherding task in the house of his father Jesse brought him low in the eyes of the members of the household, but brought him high in the eyes of God. Here it becomes clear that God's preference for the shepherd depicts his preference for the lowly, the downtrodden, and the least esteemed. As Paul wrote, he chooses

> *the foolish things of the world to shame the wise, the weak things to shame the strong, the lowly things and the despised things, and the things that are not, to nullify the things that are, so that no one may boast before him.* (1 Corinthians 1:27-29)

At the end of the day, God rejects every offering except the offering of the shepherd. If you are not willing to feed his sheep and care for his lambs—if you are not willing to bear the burdens of his people, to hold them in your heart—if you are not willing to lead them to streams of living water, God will ultimately have nothing to do with your sacrifice.

The pastoral task is not comprised of public acts of prophetic communication; the pastoral task is often hidden and secret, transpiring in the place where humility gives birth to trust, trust to transparency, and transparency to a flood of forgiveness and healing that pave the way for a new life to begin. And this way of life is not given to a select few Christians, but like the patriarchs of old, we are all called to be a pastoral people who have devoted themselves to living the pastoral lifestyle.

We are living in a day and age in which the pastoral lifestyle has once again become detestable. The rugged individualism of the western world has produced a form of Christianity that is consumerist and self-centered. While the lifestyle of the shepherd calls us to deny ourselves in order to live for others, the culture of contemporary Christianity calls us to commit ourselves to the church or ministry that provides us with the best set of personal resources and opportunities, and to maintain that commitment for as long as we find those resources to be personally fulfilling.

But the Spirit of God is moving on the hearts of his people, beckoning us back to the way of the shepherd, to the pastoral lifestyle . . . the way of the fathers of old. And it doesn't take a whole lot to answer this call; it is as simple as loving your neighbor as you love yourself, and it is the natural outflow of loving God with all of your heart, mind, and soul.

Living out the way of the shepherd is not about going to seminary, reading a lot of academic literature, or becoming any kind of an expert on any particular subject. Our overly professionalized perception of ministry gets in the way of our ability to see that God is simply calling us to *love one another deeply and from the heart* (1 Peter 1:22), to *bear one another's burdens and so fulfill the law of Christ* (Galatians 6:2), and to remain spiritual so that we can lovingly restore those who have been caught in a trespass (Galatians 6:1). The way of the shepherd is what mature love looks like when it is lived out in a community of believers.

2

Jesus the Good Shepherd

And David shepherded them with integrity of heart;
with skillful hands he led them.
(Psalm 78:72)

The Greek word for *shepherd* is *poimen*, and it occurs eighteen times in the New Testament. The root of the term is *hoiya*, which means to *protect* or *cover*. In the previous chapter we saw how important the concept of the shepherd is for understanding the Old Testament. In this chapter we will see how important the concept of the shepherd is for understanding the ministry of Jesus.

The fundamental confession of the Christian faith is that *Jesus is the Christ*, or the *Messiah*. This confession was so prominent in the early church that it very quickly became a proper name: *Jesus the Christ* became *Jesus Christ*. In acknowledging Jesus as the Christ or the Messiah, we declare him to be the long-awaited Redeemer of God's people who sits on David's throne and who will restore the kingdom to Israel. However, though this is true, we must remember that the hope for the coming of the Messiah did not fully articulate itself until the intertestamental period. When you read the Old Testament Scriptures, you do not find a clear hope for the coming of the Messiah; instead, you find the hope for the coming of the *Shepherd of Israel*:

> *For thus says the Lord God: Indeed I myself will search for my sheep and seek them out. As a shepherd seeks out his flock on the day he is among his scattered sheep, so will I seek out my sheep and deliver them from all the places where they were scattered on a cloudy and dark day.* (Ezekiel 34:11-12)

> *I will establish one shepherd over them, and he shall feed them— my servant David. He shall feed them and be their shepherd.* (Ezekiel 34:23)

> *David my servant shall be king over them, and they shall all have one shepherd; they shall also walk in my judgments and observe my statutes, and do them.* (Ezekiel 37:24)

> *But you, Bethlehem, in the land of Judah, are by no means least among the rulers of Judah; for out of you will come a ruler who will shepherd my people Israel.* (Micah 5:2; see also Matthew 2:6)

THE DAVIDIC SHEPHERD

When we think of David, the first thing that tends to come to our minds is the fact that David was the preeminent king of Israel. But before David was a king, David was a shepherd boy. The Spirit of God began to move on him, as we saw in the last chapter, when he was out in the field with his father's flocks.

When David was finally anointed king over all of Israel at Hebron, all of the people came to him and said,

> *We are your own flesh and blood. In the past while Saul was still king over us, you were the one who led Israel in their military campaigns, and the Lord said to you 'you will shepherd my people Israel and you will become their ruler.'* (2 Samuel 5:1-2)

David was Israel's conquering king, no doubt. He was also Israel's ruler and supreme authority. But his kingship, his conquest, his rule, and his authority are all spoken of in pastoral terms. *And David shepherded them with integrity of heart; with skillful hands he led them* (Psalm 78:72).

This is the foundation of the hope for the coming of the Davidic King: he would come to be the Shepherd of Israel, who would feed his people like a flock and lead them to streams of living water. The Messiah was indeed coming to be the *Davidic King*, but that meant first and foremost that he was coming to be the *Davidic Shepherd*. This identity as the shepherd was at the heart of the life and ministry of Jesus, and we can see this shepherd motif beginning to unfold itself even in the circumstances surrounding his birth.

The shepherds on the hillside are the first to hear the good news about Jesus' birth (Luke 2:8). God could have revealed the good news of his birth to anyone. The fact that he determined to reveal the gospel to a group of shepherds before revealing it to anyone else cannot be seen as an arbitrary circumstance. The angelic messengers found the shepherds watching over their flocks by night and revealed to them God's purpose in sending his Son to be the Savior of the world.

Just as Moses had to become a shepherd before he could stand before the presence of God in the bush that burned with fire and yet was not consumed, so God's revelation continues to be reserved for those who are willing to embrace the task of the shepherd. This doesn't mean that he only reveals himself to the pastoral staff of any given church. To receive revelation from God you need not embrace the pastoral title, but you do need to embrace the pastoral task. Just as God only receives the offering of the shepherd, so at the end of the day God only reveals himself to his shepherds, those who are willing to feed his sheep and care for his lambs.

The Lord shows himself to those whom he finds watching over their flocks by night. We should not expect to receive any revelation from God if we are not active participants in the task of shepherding God's flock, of restoring the broken, and of rescuing those who are heading for destruction. If you have not lifted up your voice before the Lord in prayer for one of your brothers or sisters in Christ, it is highly unlikely that God will lift up his voice to speak words of revelation to you. But if you are willing to feed God's sheep and care for his lambs, if he finds you crying out for those whom he loves in the seasons of the night, then he will most certainly open the windows of heaven over your life and show you great and mighty things which you did not know.

THE COMPASSION OF THE GOOD SHEPHERD

The compassion that Jesus exhibits in the ministry is again and again defined as a pastoral compassion. Four times the gospels tell us that Jesus moved with compassion and healed the multitudes (Matthew 9:36, 14:14; Mark 1:41, 6:34). But what was the root cause of his compassion? Was it because they were sick? Was it because they were broken?

But when he saw the multitudes, he was moved with compassion for them, because they were weary and scattered, like sheep having no shepherd. (Matthew 9:36)

I am the Good Shepherd. The Good Shepherd lays down his life for the sheep. The hired hand is not the shepherd and does not own the sheep. So when he sees the wolf coming, he abandons the sheep and runs away. Then the wolf attacks the flock and scatters it. The man runs away because he is a hired hand and cares nothing for the sheep. (John 10:11-13)

Here Jesus differentiates himself from the other leaders

of Israel by referring to them all as hired hands. The Good Shepherd functions far differently than the hired hand; when the hired hand runs and hides, the Good Shepherd stays and fights, even if it costs him his life. The Good Shepherd does not abandon the flock, but he gives his life for it.

Hired hands see their leadership as a limited task for which they expect monetary compensation. But the Good Shepherd sees his job not as a limited responsibility, but as a covenantal stewardship. The Good Shepherd does not see leadership as his opportunity to shine, to use his gifts, or to work his way up the ladder toward a bigger flock in a bigger city with a bigger salary.

The Good Shepherd does not care about applause; the Good Shepherd cares more for faithfulness than fame. And the Good Shepherd doesn't have time to rub elbows with big shots because he's too busy cleaning hooves and shearing wool. He's not looking for his one shot in which he will not miss his chance to blow,[4] he's looking for streams of living water so that his sheep don't miss their chance to drink.

As we consider these things, it is easy for us to begin to think of our leaders (whether past or present) and to begin to lament how they have not modeled the heart of the Good Shepherd for us. Regardless of who we are or where we have been, we have all had leaders who failed to emulate the model of the Good Shepherd.

But I would like to encourage us to resist this temptation.

Maintaining the heart of the Good Shepherd is not the exclusive responsibility of pastoral leaders; every member of the body of Christ is called to cultivate the heart of the Good Shepherd. This is the admonition that the apostle Paul extends to us all in saying, *Let this mind be in you which was also in Christ Jesus* (Philippians 2:5). The mind of Christ is more concerned about obedience and service than about personal opportunity, and we have all been guilty of failing to meet that standard.

The mindset of the hired hand is more concerned about authority than responsibility. For the hired hand, leadership is about the right to rule, rather than the responsibility to serve. But the mindset of the Good Shepherd is more concerned about the stewardship of souls than about the recognition of self.

THE KNOWLEDGE OF THE SHEPHERD

Jesus explained that the result of the mindset of pastoral stewardship is spiritual intimacy. *I am the Good Shepherd*, said Jesus. *I know my sheep and my sheep know me* (John 10:14). Again, in verse 27 he says, *My sheep listen to my voice; I know them and they follow me*. Intimacy is the mark of the relationship between a shepherd and a flock. The shepherd knows the flock and knows it intimately, so much so that he can tell his sheep and the sheep of another flock in an instant.

In ancient Israel, two shepherds would often spend the night together in a cave, and both flocks would mingle in the cave with them. They would light a fire, they'd have dinner, and their flocks would all be mingling together. They wouldn't stop and say "Wait, let me put a tag on all of my sheep so that I will be able to tell them apart in the morning!" They would spend the night together and in the morning there would never be a question as to whose sheep was whose. The shepherds knew each sheep so well that they could immediately say, "I know this one. I don't know this one." It was pastoral language that Jesus used in Matthew 7:23 when he spoke of those to whom he would one day say, "I never knew you."

Sheep are not very intelligent animals, but they do have an uncanny ability to learn the voice of their shepherd and to hear it above every other voice. Jesus said of his sheep, *They will never follow a stranger. In fact they will run away from him because they do not recognize a stranger's voice* (John 10:5).

Jesus further explained that the role of the shepherd is to function as a gate for the sheep. *I tell you the truth, I am the gate for the sheep*, Jesus said (John 10:7). Then in verses 9 and 10 he said:

> *I am the gate; whoever enters through me will be saved. He will come in and go out and find pasture. The thief comes only to steal to kill and to destroy. But I am come that they may have life and that they might have it to the full.*

The point is that thieves enter the flock to fleece it—to use it for their own means and to cast it aside when they are done with it. The Good Shepherd enters the flock not to take from it, but to give to it. The Good Shepherd is a gate. The Good Shepherd gives everything but takes nothing because he needs nothing from the sheep. Jesus is the only shepherd who does not feed on his flock, but instead invites his flock to feed on him. Instead of sacrificing the members of his flock for his own well-being, he sacrifices his own well-being for the members of his flock in order that they might have life.

This is the heart of Jesus, the Good Shepherd, and we are called to let this heart be in us as well. When we see this heart of Jesus, we are not simply to admire it, but to acquire it. And the acquisition of the heart of Christ requires us to do away with the distinction between our personal walks with Christ and our passionate desire to care for his people. To love Jesus is to love what he loves, and to love what he loves requires the embrace of the pastoral task.

This explains the encounter between Jesus and Peter on the Sea of Galilee after the resurrection, when Jesus prepared breakfast for Peter on the shore (John 21:15-17). There Jesus motions toward the fish that Peter had just caught and asks him a very pointed question: *"Simon son of John, do you love me more than these?"* Peter immediately and vigorously responds in the affirmative: *"Yes, Lord, you know that I love you."* Jesus replies, *"Feed my lambs."* To paraphrase, he is saying, "Peter, do you love me? If you love me, you've got to be willing to take care of my sheep. You can't say that you love me unless you love what I love, and if you love what I love, then your heart will yearn to feed my lambs and take care of my sheep!"

Whenever we read this passage it is easy for us to miss the fact that here Jesus makes it impossible for Peter to embrace Jesus without embracing the way of the shepherd. You cannot embrace the Good Shepherd while rejecting the way of the Good Shepherd; "if you love me," Jesus says, "then you've got to be willing to feed my sheep!"

But many of us in the body of Christ believe that we can do just that; we think we can run into the loving arms of Jesus while simultaneously running away from the pastoral task. We love to sing and even serve, but we don't want anything to do with the stewardship of souls! And this distinction does not simply indicate a lack of value for pastoral ministry; it indicates a lack of mature love for Jesus!

Despite this, I believe that the Church is on the verge of a new awakening of love for Jesus that will compel us into the heart of the pastoral task. And the sign of that awakening is the explosive desire for the discovery and fulfillment of destiny that is emerging within the body of Christ. The people of God, like never before, have awakened to the fact that every member of the body of Christ has a distinct destiny in God, that all of God's people are anointed, gifted, and called by God to accomplish great things.

At the same time, the vast majority of believers are feeling frustrated and anxious about their ability to discover and fulfill that destiny. Many members of the body of Christ are frustrated, and they can't figure out why they are frustrated. They have a sense of what God has called them to do, but they can't figure out why the fulfillment of it is so elusive.

What is missing is a clear understanding of the fact that in order to discover and fulfill your destiny, you must be willing to enroll in the school of the shepherd. Rejecting the pastoral task is a decision that will distance you from your destiny. And the perpetual rejection of that task is tantamount to the perpetual postponement of your destiny.

Just as Moses must have seen no connection between the task of shepherding the flocks of Jethro and the calling to deliver Israel from bondage, so the average believer tends to see no connection between simple tasks (like leading a small group or encouraging a new believer) and the fulfillment of grand hopes and dreams for the future. But the connection is clear. Loving Jesus compels you to love his people. Loving his people qualifies you to lead his people. And leading his people catapults you to the fulfillment of your destiny in God.

3

The Ministry of the Spiritual

*You lead your people like a flock by the hand
of Moses and Aaron.*
(Psalm 77:20)

In Galatians 6:1, Paul admonishes those who are
"spiritual" to gently restore those who have been overtaken by a
trespass. Notice that Paul does not say, *you who are pastors.*
Instead, he says *you who are spiritual.* The ministry of restoration
is not exclusive to the pastor, but rightly resides within the
purview of all who demonstrate proficiency in the life of the
Spirit.

When someone is caught in a trespass, it doesn't take an
office-holder of the church to restore him to peace and purity;
all it takes is one who is spiritual—a brother or sister in Christ
who cares enough about the person to take him by the hand and

lead him back to his place of wholeness in Christ by the power of the Spirit.

More than ever before, the body of Christ is in need of the ministry of the *spiritual*. More than ever before, the children of God are finding themselves caught in the grip of trespasses and sins that clutch the soul with the intent of destroying it. But by and large when the everyday Christian sees a brother who has been caught in a trespass, he does not think he has the power to restore him. Instead, he encourages him to go talk to his pastor.

It is time for the church to wake up and realize that when a brother is caught in a trespass, he doesn't necessarily need a pastor; he needs the *pastoral*. All he needs is a brother or sister who is spiritual enough to see past the pit he has fallen into and who loves him enough to take the time to lift him out of it. And Paul tells us here in Galatians 6 that this blessed pastoral task belongs to all who are spiritual.

DEFINING THE SPIRITUAL

What does it mean to be spiritual? The word in the Greek is *pneumatikos* and it means *of the Spirit*. To be *of the Spirit* can be described in three different ways.

First, it means to live *from the Spirit*, which means that the Spirit is the source from which you draw your strength, hope, joy, wisdom, peace, power, and knowledge. To live *from the Spirit* means that you are continually depending upon the presence of the Holy Spirit as the source of power in your daily life.

The alternative to living from the Spirit is living from the flesh. Those who live from the flesh are self-dependent instead of Spirit-dependent. In Romans 8, Paul juxtaposes the life that is lived *according to the Spirit* (*kata pneuma*) with the life that is lived *according to the flesh* (*kata sarka*).

> *For those who live according to the flesh set their minds on the things of the flesh, but those who live according to the Spirit, the things of the Spirit* (Romans 8:5).

He then goes on to describe the trajectories of each orientation: *For to be carnally minded is death, but to be spiritually minded is life and peace* (Romans 8:6).

Those who are *of* the Spirit have learned how to live *from* the Spirit, and because they have learned to live from the Spirit, their lives naturally begin to reflect the character of the Spirit. Since the Spirit is always at peace, those who are spiritual (to the degree that they are able to remain spiritual) are also always at peace. And since the Spirit is always vibrantly alive, those who are spiritual are also always vibrantly alive.

Second, to be spiritual also means to live *by the Spirit*, which means that the Spirit is the Person who directs the lives of the spiritually minded. Those who live according to the flesh are not only self-dependent, but self-motivated: they go wherever they want to go and do whatever they want to do. But those who live according to the Spirit are Spirit-motivated: they go wherever the Spirit wants them to go and they do whatever the Spirit wants them to do.

Those who are spiritual are often found saying *no* when the world says *yes*, and saying *yes* when the world says *no*. They walk away from doors that the world opens for them and they wait patiently before doors that God promises to open for them. Those who are spiritual do not live to take advantage of every opportunity for personal gain. Instead, they live for the glory of Jesus: they long to do his will, reflect his glory, and increase his fame.

Because those who are spiritual are led by the Spirit, rather than by their own desires, their lives are characterized by the supernatural intervention of God. If we were to carefully examine the lives of those who live by the Spirit, we would find the Spirit leading them from victory to victory and from glory to glory. While in the natural it might seem that the spiritual miss out on great opportunities, upon examination we would find that for every opportunity they forsake for the Spirit's sake they receive a hundredfold return in blessing and glory.

Finally, to be spiritual also means to live *toward the Spirit*, which means that the Spirit is not only the source of the lives of the spiritual, but the goal of their lives as well. The Spirit is himself the reward of the spiritual. Their desire is not simply to go forth from him in obedience to him, but to delve into the depths of the life of the Spirit, where he begins to reveal to them the deep things of God. In the Spirit, the spiritual begin to partake of the revelation of Jesus, gaze upon the eternal love of the Father, and drink deeply from the well of salvation.

This is what it means to be spiritual. But it does not describe what it means to *become* spiritual. Those who are spiritual have not always been spiritual; in fact, the cultivation of the spiritual life is often facilitated by the intentional turning away from a life of foolishness and carnality. Since our weaknesses are the result of the affliction of our souls, our weaknesses become opportunities for God to present himself to us as the Good Shepherd, bringing his transforming power and love right into the place of our shortcomings.

God always chooses the weak things of this world to confound the strong and the foolish things to confound the wise (1 Corinthians 1:27). Why does he do this? Because when he chooses a weak and rejected thing, he hardwires trust as a necessity into its very being. When Moses was confident, God had to humble him; when Moses had no confidence, that's when God came to empower him. This is the great paradox of leadership in the kingdom of God; if you are strong, he makes you weak so that he can give you true strength, and if you are weak, he makes you strong so that you can lift up those who are weak.

The mark of the spiritual life is compassionate love. The spiritual have the emotional space to minister to those who have fallen into a trespass without judgment or condemnation because they are always cognizant of the depths from which their own souls have been drawn by the mercy of the Lord. It is the love of Christ that compels the spiritual man or woman to engage in the ministry of restoration, and it is the love of Christ that procures victory in this endeavor, because love never fails.

We enter the pastoral lifestyle by way of compassionate love, and yet we only become fruitful there by way the demonstration of divine power. Divine love always demands a demonstration of divine power. Some of us are content to walk in a powerless form of divine love, and others of us are content to walk in a loveless form of divine power. But both methods are failures to walk in the way of the Good Shepherd, for his way is laden with both love and power.

By and large, the everyday believer embraces a powerless form of divine love. We know that Jesus commanded us to love God and love one another; this is clearly intended for every believer. But the power of God, so we think, is not something that every believer needs to be concerned about. When the everyday believer speaks of his relationship with the power of God, it is typically in regard to personal change or personal benefit. Testimonies of how God changed "me" from the inside out, or about how God provided for "me" in miraculous ways abound among believers. But very rarely do you hear a believer testify about how God used her to set someone else free!

This is because the everyday believer has yet to embrace the pastoral task as her own. The average believer thinks pastoring is for pastors and the power of God is reserved for the office-holders of the church. But this way of thinking is completely wrong and misguided.

The whole body of Christ is called to participate in the pastoral task. We are called to be a pastoral people, and that means every member of the body of Christ is called to demonstrate both divine love and divine power.

Love and power are often experienced as counterpoint realities . . . at times we find our hearts overflowing with one to the neglect of the other. To be a deliverer requires power, but to be a shepherd requires love. When Moses first presented himself as Israel's would-be deliverer, he possessed a sense of power that was devoid of love. In the wilderness, God wedded love and power together within Moses' being.

THE SPIRITUAL SHEPHERD SUPERNATURALLY

During his time in the wilderness, Moses learned not only how to deliver Israel, but how to shepherd Israel. And he led them not according to human wisdom, not according to human knowledge, not according to current trends and practices, but by receiving instruction from the Lord and obeying it. And in doing so, his pastoral ministry demonstrated supernatural power: the power of deliverance from captivity, of protection from disaster, of mobility in the place of restriction, of provision in famine. Moses learned early on that God, not he, was the deliverer of his people, and his continual dependence upon the power of God was what facilitated the demonstration of this reality.

Because Moses shepherded supernaturally, the people of Israel could clearly see that God was their shepherd and that Moses was simply his instrument, leading them generations later to cry out to God rather than Moses:

Hear us, O Shepherd of Israel. You who lead Joseph like a flock, you who sit enthroned between the cherubim, shine forth between Ephraim, Benjamin, and Manasseh. Awaken your might; come and save us. (Psalm 80:1)

Israel saw in the shepherding ministry of Moses the shepherding ministry of God . . . but only because Moses shepherded supernaturally. What happened through the ministry of Moses went far beyond the wisdom, knowledge, and understanding that a human being could possibly possess. This continual demonstration of supernatural power was proof to Israel that God was truly their shepherd.

The psalmist acknowledges this when he prays, *You lead your people like a flock by the hand of Moses and Aaron* (Psalm 77:20). In the next chapter, the psalmist says, *He brought his people out like a flock. He led them like sheep through the desert* (78:52). This clearly depicts God's leadership over his people in the wilderness during their forty years of wandering. Even after Moses died, God said he was still going to lead his people like a flock. This is the foundation of the confident cry of the psalmist that we find in Psalm 80:1 (see above).

We established in the last chapter that the whole body of

Christ is called to participate in the pastoral task, not just those deemed pastors. This also means that all of God's children must be zealous for the supernatural intervention of God in and through their lives. If we are going to participate in the pastoral task of leading God's people to springs of living water, the people we lead must know that through us God is leading them and not we by our own power.

If your pastoral ministry demonstrates no supernatural power, the people you serve will inadvertently begin to trust you to be their shepherd. But if your pastoral ministry demonstrates the supernatural power of God, then the people will always know that it is God who is their shepherd, and they will trust him to be their guide. When we do not shepherd supernaturally, people build up a dependency upon us. But the moment the supernatural power of God begins to flow through our ministries, people's eyes begin to turn upward, toward the Lord. This conviction is clearly communicated by Paul in 1 Corinthians 2:

My message and my preaching did not come through wise words of human wisdom, but in demonstration of the Spirit's power so that your faith might not rest in the wisdom of man, but in the power of God. (1 Corinthians 2:4-5)

The demonstration of the Spirit's power through Paul's ministry convinced the people of Corinth that there was something more than Paul going on there. The demonstration of

God's power through Moses' ministry convinced the people of Israel that there was something more than Moses going on there. And if we are going to minister in the name of the Shepherd of Israel, the demonstration of the Spirit's power must convince the people we serve that there is something more than us going on here. Thus the cry for the demonstration of divine power is a key attribute of the genuine shepherd's heart.

As Moses approached the end of his days, his heart began to cry out for the Lord to set a true shepherd over the house of Israel so that the end of the pastoral ministry of Moses would not spell the end of God's pastoral ministry to his people. And his description of that shepherd speaks volumes to us about the true nature of the pastoral task:

> *May the Lord, the God who gives breath to all living things, appoint someone over this community to go out and come in before them, one who will lead them out and bring them in, so the Lord's people will not be like sheep without a shepherd.* (Numbers 28:16-18)

I think I might have prayed a completely different prayer. *Lord, we need somebody who can preach up in here! Otherwise the people will start leaving! And please make sure that the person whom you appoint has a good grasp of church history, exegetical method, and systematic theology!* But Moses only lists two qualifications for the leader in question. First, the shepherd needs to be able to *go out and come in before them* (or *in full view of them*), which means that he can model the lifestyle that he preaches. Next, he's got to be willing and able to *lead them out and bring them in*, which means that he must be willing and able to bear the responsibility of teaching the people of Israel how to live before the Lord.

> *So the Lord said to Moses, "Take Joshua son of Nun, a man in whom is the spirit of leadership, and lay your hand on him."* (Numbers 27:18)

What Moses imparted to Joshua was not a list of principles for successful ministry, or a collection of timeless truths for the journey. What Moses imparted to Joshua was the heart of a shepherd, who would go out and come in before the people of God and lead them out and bring them in. These qualities are more about the heart of the shepherd than they are about the skill-set of the shepherd.

THE PURPOSE OF THE PASTORAL

This description of the ministry of the shepherd is much more organic than the typical description of the work of the modern-day pastor. The most popular way to define the work of a pastor in our day and age is by enumerating the activities which comprise the weekly schedule of the pastor: preaching, teaching, counseling, planning, administrating, etc. This way of defining the ministry of the pastor focuses on pastoral activities, rather than the pastoral purpose.

You know that pastors are supposed to preach, but have you ever stopped to ask why? You know that pastors are supposed to teach, but why? Why do they counsel, plan, and administrate? The answers to these questions are not even clear to those of us who have given our lives to full-time pastoral ministry. Often we can have a clear understanding of the activities we are supposed to be engaged in, but be completely confused about what those activities are supposed to accomplish.

I certainly experienced this in my early days as a church planter. In the absence of clarity, I found myself trying to function as a therapist, a life-coach, a motivational speaker, a comedian, an advisor, a Bible communicator . . . the list goes on. While there is nothing inherently wrong with any of these functions, I never felt fully satisfied with what my activities produced.

What I came to discover is that the true task of the pastor is to shepherd the soul. All of the pastoral activities we may engage in are mere tools designed to aid us in this true task. But before we go further, we must first stop to consider the nature of the soul itself. We cannot begin to shepherd the soul until we first understand what it is. In order to answer this question, we must go back beyond the wilderness to the Garden of Eden, where God created humankind in his own image and likeness. To this we turn in the next chapter.

4

The Anatomy of the Soul

And the Lord God formed man of the dust of the ground, and
breathed into his nostrils the breath of life;
and man became a living soul.

(Genesis 2:7)

As mentioned in the last chapter, before we delve into the particulars of the task of shepherding the soul, we must first stop to consider the nature of the soul itself, as God created it in the Garden of Eden.

In Genesis we can perceive a clear distinction between the way in which God creates humankind and the way in which he brings forth the rest of creation. The heavens and the earth and the sea and all that is in them he creates from a distance by simply sending forth the word of his command. But when he creates Adam, he comes down into creation and forms Adam out of the dust of the ground.

The *modus operandi* of creation illustrates the purpose of creation. God *creates* (*barah*) the earth and the animals from afar by sending his word because they are created simply to obey his command. But when he creates Adam he gets down on his hands and knees in the dust, and he *forms* (*yatsar*) him in his own image and likeness. While the earth and animals are created from afar, Adam is created face to face.

THE SPIRIT OF LIFE

And God formed the man (adam) out of the dust of the ground (adamah) (Genesis 2:7). Adam emerges out of *adamah*, and he is nothing more than a dust figurine–a sort of divine origami–until God puts his mouth over Adam's nose and breathes into his nostrils the breath of life: *and Adam became a living soul* (Genesis 2:7).

Here we must stop and remember that salvation in Christ is the effective reversal of all that went wrong in the Garden of Eden. In Christ, we are restored to the fellowship that Adam and Eve lost because of sin. This means that every component of our redemption has a corollary in the Garden.

With that in mind it becomes significant to notice that the phrase *breath of life* can also be translated *spirit of life*. God breathed into his nostrils the spirit of life—the same Spirit of life which, in Christ Jesus, sets us free from the law of sin and of death (Romans 8:2). The gift of the Holy Spirit is given to us in redemption because it was lost in the Fall. Adam became a living soul not simply because God gave him the ability to breathe; Adam became a living soul because God gave him the gift of the Holy Spirit!

Think about this for a moment: Adam became a human being at the moment God gave him the gift of the Spirit. In Adam's first moment of consciousness he was full of the Holy Spirit and in a face to face encounter with God. This is what it means to be human! To be human means to be a living soul, and to be a living soul means to be filled with the Spirit and in a face to face encounter with God.

Now we can understand why Adam and Eve didn't drop dead the moment they ate of the tree of the knowledge of good and evil. Remember, God promised them that on the day they ate of it they would surely die. Why didn't they drop dead? Because God was not speaking of biological death, but of the death of the soul.

This is why Paul speaks of our being dead in our trespasses and sins prior to coming to Christ. This spiritual death began the moment Adam and Eve ate from the tree. They did die immediately, but it was the death of their souls and not their bodies. And the sign of their immediate spiritual death was the experience of shame and fear, the desire to run and hide both from each other and from God, and the strategy of blaming God, each other, and the devil when confronted with their sin. None of these things would have been possible for them at the moment of their creation. But now the gift of the Spirit has departed and they have suffered the death of their souls.

This is why Ezekiel declares that *the soul that sins shall die* (Ezekiel 18:20), and why James says, *If anyone turns a sinner away from the error of his ways, he will save a soul from death* (James 5:20). A few verses earlier he says, *All souls are mine* (Ezekiel 18:4). The truth declared here is that the human soul was created to be God's possession and the satisfaction of the soul depends upon it existing in a place of divine possession. If your soul is not possessed by God, it is not satisfied.

In Numbers 21, when the children of Israel were grumbling against God and Moses, one of their chief complaints was the tastelessness of the manna. God rained manna down from heaven for them, but in Numbers 21:5, they cried out, *Our soul loathes this tasteless bread*. It was the soul that loathed it. When you eat food that's good for you, your body likes it, but your soul hates it because it doesn't create the kind of experiential delight created by unhealthy foods. Delight takes place in the soul. Desire takes place in the soul. Need takes place in the soul:

> *It shall even be as when a hungry man dreams, and look—he eats; but he awakes, and his soul is still empty; or as when a thirsty man dreams, And look—he drinks; But he awakes, and indeed he is faint, And his soul still craves.* (Isaiah 29:8)

It's the soul that's empty; it's the soul that craves. Proverbs 27:7 says, *A satisfied soul loathes the honeycomb, but to a hungry soul, every bitter thing is sweet*. And Ecclesiastes 6:7 says, *All the labor of a man is for his mouth, yet his soul is not satisfied*.

The pervasive predicament of the human soul is the experience of emptiness and dissatisfaction, and the source of that dissatisfaction was Eve's decision to entertain the lies of the serpent in eating that which God had commanded her not to eat, and Adam's subsequent committal of that same sin.

FULLNESS & LIFE

The enemy comes not but for to steal, to kill and to destroy, said Jesus (John 10:10). What did the enemy come to steal, kill, and destroy? He didn't come to steal any material possessions from Adam and Eve. Neither did he come to kill them physically. Neither did he come to destroy the order of the Garden of Eden. Instead, he came to steal the gift of life that had been deposited in their souls, to kill their life-giving connection to God and to one another, and to destroy the peace and prosperity of soul they enjoyed by virtue of the indwelling Spirit who facilitated their ongoing fellowship with the Father.

I have come that they might have life, and that they might have it to the full (John 10:10). It's interesting that Jesus uses the third person, *they*. Who are *they*? I think *they* refers to Adam and Eve. Jesus came to reverse the curse of soul-death that transpired in the Garden via the sin of Adam and Eve.

When Jesus says he has come that we might have life, he is talking about the life of the soul. And when he says he has come that we might have it to the full, he is alluding to the fact that the soul longs for fullness . . . that *fullness* and *life* are synonymous to the soul. The death of the soul is equivalent to its emptiness. This is why, as Augustine says, *The heart is restless till it finds its rest in [God]*,[5] and Blaise Paschal speaks in his *Pensées* of the "infinite abyss" within the soul that "can be filled only with an infinite and immutable object."[6]

You will fill me with joy in your presence; with everlasting pleasures at your right hand (Psalm 16:11), says the psalmist of God. This fullness of joy and eternal pleasure is what the soul was created for. But when it wanders off like a stray sheep, it finds itself bereft and alone, groping for joy, peace, and hope, and finding nothing more than cheap counterfeits and poor substitutes in the pleasures of the world. This is why we must be diligent to return to Jesus, the Shepherd and Overseer of our souls (1 Peter 2:25).

But what does it mean for the soul to wander off like a stray sheep? And what does it mean for the soul to return to its Shepherd and Overseer? In order to answer these questions, we must consider the question of the constitution of the soul. The soul is comprised of the mind, the will, and the emotions. This means that the three core functions of the soul are thinking, feeling, and deciding. The soul wanders away from Jesus when with the mind it forsakes his truth, with the heart it abandons his love, and with the will it disregards his commands. And the soul returns to Jesus when with the mind it embraces his truth, with the heart it revels in his love, and with the will it follows his commands.

However, the soul is not able to make this move on its own; as we see in Psalm 23, when the soul is afflicted, it needs a shepherd. When the soul embraces the Lord as its Shepherd in the midst of its affliction, he leads it beside still waters, makes it lie down in green pastures, leads it in paths of righteousness, and restores it. And this last statement is the most remarkable at this point, for here the psalmist uses the Hebrew word *shuv* to describe the restorative process of the Lord. *He restores (shuv) my soul.* The term *shuv* means literally to *turn* or *repent*. The psalmist says, *He turns my soul.* When I'm not able to turn my soul by my own power, he turns my soul. When I'm not able to make my soul repent by my own power, he repents my soul. What a remarkable statement!

THE SOUL MUST CHOOSE A SHEPHERD

However, as stated before, the Lord is not the only shepherd who is presented to the soul in the moment of its affliction. At the moment in which the soul is afflicted, another shepherd also appears. That shepherd is the flesh and it beckons to us through the mouth of its prophet, pleasure. Pleasure does not offer to heal or restore the soul; it simply offers to momentarily relieve the soul of its affliction by giving it a temporary escape from its pain. But what pleasure does not divulge to the soul is the fact that it will lead it down a path of ever-deepening pain and destruction. Pleasure offers itself as a free gift to the soul, but in reality the soul must pay a hefty price for its flight into the realm of worldly pleasure. For the soul that has tasted the goodness of God, the aftertaste of worldly pleasure is as bitter as gall. This is what Paul means when he says that *the wages of sin is death.*

In the moment of its affliction, the soul must choose its shepherd. The soul stands in the moment of affliction at a great divide, and the choice it makes in this crucial moment will determine the character of its destiny. In Romans 8, Paul describes the crisis of choice encountered by the soul in the moment of its affliction in terms of the decision either to walk in the flesh or to walk in the Spirit:

> *For those who live according to the flesh set their minds on the things of the flesh, but those who live according to the Spirit, the things of the Spirit. For to be carnally minded is death, but to be spiritually minded is life and peace. Because the carnal mind is enmity against God; for it is not subject to the law of God, nor indeed can be. So then, those who are in the flesh cannot please God. (Romans 8:5-8)*

When the soul turns toward the flesh in the moment of its affliction, it repeats the error of Adam and Eve in the Garden and returns to the outcome of that error. To be carnally minded is death . . . The term *carnal* literally means *fleshly,* and the realm of the flesh is simply the realm of dependence upon human strength in isolation from God. The mind becomes carnal when it retreats from the truth of God and decides to lean upon its own understanding. But the mind becomes spiritual when it sets itself upon the things that the Spirit desires.

The mind is the lead member of the soul; wherever the mind goes, the heart follows, and wherever the heart goes, the will follows, and wherever the will goes, the body follows. Feelings are the products of thoughts and decisions are the product of feelings. The body is at the back of this parade and simply follows the trajectory set for it by the soul. If we can get our minds right, we can change virtually every other component of our lives!

This truth is so profound and necessary for the body of Christ right now because we are witnessing a mass proliferation of spiritual and emotional maladies in this time that are plaguing the people of God. And the body of Christ is crying out for a solution. The body of Christ is at this very moment experiencing a dire crisis of soul. Even the strongest and most prolific among us seem to be falling prey to the devices of the evil one, and so many of us feel that there is virtually nothing we can do to stop it.

But there is something we can do! We can learn how to embrace the ministry of Jesus, the Good Shepherd . . . we can learn how to spur one another on toward love and good works. And we can become skillful in the art of shepherding the soul!

Just think about it: James says that if you turn a sinner

away from the error of his ways, you save a soul from death (James 5:20). How powerful is that? To think that if you get a hold of this ministry of the Good Shepherd, you can do more than lead people in the sinner's prayer at the bus stop . . . you can actually turn sinners away from the error of their ways and save many souls from death!

But we must begin by acknowledging that we have not done so well in this area in recent years. By and large, the body of Christ does not know how to gently restore those who have fallen; instead, we harshly condemn them. And once we have harshly condemned them, we don't know how to receive them with meekness; instead, we send them away in shame. However, all of that can change if we begin to get a hold of the ministry of the Good Shepherd!

In the pages that follow, I will take the components of the soul one by one and reflect upon what it means for each component to participate in the ministry of the Good Shepherd.

5

The Logic of the Serpent

Do not be conformed to the pattern of this age, but be transformed by the renewing of your mind.
(Romans 12:2)

In this chapter we begin a series of discussions on exactly how the soul can be shepherded. We will begin with the mind because the mind is the lead member of the soul, and it follows that the effective shepherding of the soul begins with knowing how to appropriately deal with the mind. This, admittedly, is a daunting proposition, because the mind is the most stubborn thing to deal with. We know this not only from dealing with the minds of others, but from dealing with our own minds as well.

The New Testament teaches us that unless the mind is renewed and transformed, it is God's enemy. *The carnal mind*, says Paul, *is enmity against God, for it is not subject to the law of God, nor indeed can be* (Romans 8:7). The term *carnal* here is a translation of the Greek *sarkikos*, which literally means *of the flesh*. Here we understand that it is not simply the mind that is

God's enemy, but the mind of the flesh.

The mind of the flesh can be defined as thinking in isolation from God. When we have "thought parties" that God is not invited to, the thought processes produced at these "parties" are carnal in nature. The carnal mind is the mind left to its own devices, disconnected from its divine source, and led toward conclusions that diverge from the truth of the word of God. But the key to understanding the power of the carnal mind is the recognition that its origins are demonic.

THE BIRTH OF THE CARNAL MIND

The carnal mind was born in the Garden of Eden on the day Eve had a conversation with a serpent. The serpent's strategy was to lead her down a logic trail that disconnected her from the command of God. The end result was that she began to think for herself . . . so she thought. She had a thought party that God was not invited to, but what she failed to realize was that she had allowed Satan to attend. Her train of thought was not simply natural; it was demonic.

Satan led her down this path first by asking a question: *Did God really say . . . ?* Then he makes a suggestion: *You will not surely die . . .* Finally, he levels an accusation: *The Lord knows that on the day you eat of it you will become like him.* Once Eve entertained the question she was susceptible to the suggestion, and once she entertained the suggestion, she was susceptible to the accusation, and once she entertained the accusation, she was completely deceived and was no longer subject to the law of God —the command not to eat of the tree.

It was at this point that the tree became desirable to Eve. Before the serpent led her down this logic trail, she knew only one thing about the tree: God had commanded her not to eat of it. But now that the logic of the serpent had succeeded in disconnecting her mind from the command of God, she actually began to desire the thing that was repulsive to her just a moment prior.

So when the woman saw that the tree was good for food, that it was pleasant to the eyes, and a tree desirable to make one wise, she took of its fruit and ate. (Genesis 3:6)

When we think about it, the situation created by the carnal mind is quite unusual. Eve knew that God had commanded her not to eat of the tree, but then she gained a different perspective regarding the nature of the thing God had commanded her not to eat. She thought she had become enlightened, but in reality she had been deceived. And once she was deceived, lust was conceived and brought forth sin.

This is the character of the carnal mind. When we are operating in the carnal mind, we not only disagree with God's perspective on the outcome of our actions, but we actually desire the very things that God has clearly commanded us not to touch. The carnal mind emboldens us to critique the explicit will of God and to contradict it with our actions because the carnal mind is bent on disobedience and is beyond remediation.

This being the case, we must recognize from the outset that we cannot win an argument with someone who is operating in the carnal mind. The hallmark of the carnal mind is rebellion that defies all reason. If you don't realize this, you're going to be frustrated continually when the people that you try to minister to turn you around and around in circles and refuse to surrender even when there's nowhere for them to go. You can give them every reason in the book and they will still pretend that they don't see or understand the truth.

When you're trying to convince a husband who has cheated on his wife that none of the excuses that he is offering up for his infidelity are valid, you're dealing with the carnal mind. When you're trying to convince a friend to release her unforgiveness and reconcile with her brother or sister, you're dealing with the carnal mind. And when you're trying to convince a brother or sister that there are plenty of people who love and care for him and that he is not rejected and insignificant, you are typically dealing with the carnal mind.

THE OPERATIONS OF THE CARNAL MIND

The fundamental operation of the carnal mind is creating a rational justification for impending sin. This is exactly what happened with Eve. The goal of the serpent was to get her to eat the fruit and disobey God. The strategy of the serpent was to construct a logic trail for her that would justify the action in her own mind. When it comes to constructing rational justifications for the decision to sin, the carnal mind is incredibly creative! It has the power to generate the most convincing arguments on the fly. Some of the most prolific among them are worth noting.

First, there's the argument of biological necessity: *The Lord knows I need this, and since he has not provided it for me, I guess it's okay for me to take it for myself.* Then there's the argument of emotional deprivation: *Nobody cares about me anyway . . . not even God!* There's also the argument of reciprocal justice: *Well, he did it to me first, so if I do it back to him I'm well within my rights!* The list can go on and on, and as soon as you renounce one of these arguments, the carnal mind seems to just conjure up another. And when you are in the flesh, the arguments of the carnal mind are exceedingly compelling!

The subsequent operation of the carnal mind is the refusal to take personal responsibility for the sin committed. When God confronted Adam and Eve after they had eaten from the tree of the knowledge of good and evil, they both immediately began to shift blame away from themselves. Adam blamed God and Eve: *The woman you gave me . . .* and Eve blamed the devil: *The serpent gave me and I did eat.* When we are in the flesh, we either blame the people around us who have failed to love us as we *deserve* to be loved, or we blame the devil. This is because the carnal mind is skillful not only in providing us with the justification that we need in order to sin against God, but the excuses that we need to continue our quest for satisfaction in isolation from him.

The sign that we have come back into the realm of the Spirit is repentance. When we repent, we take full responsibility for our actions, acknowledging that our thinking has become futile and resolving to renounce the questions, suggestions, and accusations of the enemy and return to the truth of the Shepherd and Overseer of our souls.

But the question remains: how do we lead people to the place of repentance when they are clearly operating in the carnal mind? When we see brothers or sisters who are rationalizing and then justifying, how do we convince them to turn from the error of their ways and return to the Shepherd and Overseer of their souls?

The first key to dealing with the machinations of the carnal mind is to understand that you cannot reason with it. The carnal mind cannot be reformed; it can only be renewed as the old man is put to death and the new man comes alive. You cannot logically reason someone into a place of surrender and repentance when their thinking has gone astray. If you try, you'll find yourself in a quagmire of foolishness. A particular exhortation of Paul's to his beloved son Timothy comes to mind here:

> *But avoid foolish and ignorant disputes, knowing that they generate strife. And a servant of the Lord must not quarrel, but be gentle to all, able to teach, patient, in humility correcting*

those who are in opposition, if God perhaps will grant them repentance, so that they may know the truth, and that they may come to their senses and escape the snare of the devil, having been taken captive by him to do his will. (2 Timothy 2:23-26)

You cannot argue with the carnal mind. You cannot engage it on its own terms. And you cannot persuade people who are operating in the carnal mind to turn from the error of their ways. Instead, you must gently and humbly offer them instruction in the hopes that God will grant them repentance. When a person is not voluntarily repentant, the only hope for bringing them back to the place of repentance is God's sovereign intervention, and the only way to facilitate the possibility of divine intervention in this situation is to offer patient and humble instruction.

But you must exercise discernment in the process; the fact that you have discerned the operations of the carnal mind does not mean that you should speak to it immediately. There is a divine *kairos* (opportune time) for instruction and correction that you must discern in order to maximize the potential for repentance to transpire. Note what Proverbs has to say on the matter:

Do not answer a fool according to his folly,
Lest you also be like him.
Answer a fool according to his folly,
Lest he be wise in his own eyes. (Proverbs 26:4-5)

The first proverb says *do not answer a fool* and the second says *answer a fool*. Which is it? In order to answer that question you must have discernment. There is a time and place for simply rebuking foolishness with your silence—refusing to say a word in response to the articulated logic of the carnal mind. Sometimes the best thing you can do is simply stand still and silent in the presence of one who is spouting forth carnal nonsense (and if and when you do so, you must resist the urge to nod your head in empathetic agreement).

But when and if the time is right, you can and should speak directly to the foolishness of the carnal mind with the control of a gentle firmness. I can think of several times in my life when people have done this for me, and it is very powerful—and it is not something that only a pastor can do. Sometimes it is even more powerful when a brother or sister smiles at you and says, lovingly yet firmly, *What you just said is not accurate at all.*

THE PRINCIPLE OF EXPEDIENCE

I can think of one occasion in which Jesus did this for Peter. Jesus had just informed his disciples that he was about to be handed over to the Gentiles and put to death, and Peter responded by taking Jesus aside and rebuking him. Jesus simply looked at Peter and said, *Get behind me Satan, you are a hindrance to me; for you do not consider the things of God, but the things of man* (Matthew 16:23). That may sound pretty gangster, but that is exactly what Peter needed at that moment to shake him free from the carnal foolishness he had allowed his heart to entertain.

The principle is expedience. The question is not what is the right thing to say when you are dealing with the carnal mind; the question is what does the individual you are dealing with need to hear in order to break free from the bondage of deception? The answer to that question is different for different people. Some people are so sensitive that if you were ever to rebuke them harshly you'd break them permanently. And other people are so thick-skinned that unless you punch them in the stomach as hard as you can (figuratively speaking), they'll never have a chance of returning to their senses.

I dealt with a man once who was going to leave his wife and their newborn baby for little to no reason at all. I tried to reason with him at first, but saw that I was getting nowhere. So I got up in his face, pointed my finger right at his nose, and raised my voice at him with all of the severity and intensity I could muster. My wife saw this go down and felt so uncomfortable that she got on her knees and began to pray. But after it was over the man called me on the phone and thanked me, saying that no one had ever loved him enough to get in his face like that.

The thing that you must realize is that when you are dealing with the carnal mind, you are dealing with rebellion beyond reason, and when you are dealing with rebellion beyond reason, you are dealing with the phenomenon known as foolishness. Foolishness has two potential sources.

The first source of foolishness is the heart of a child.

Sometimes the foolishness that we exhibit doesn't come from a heart that is bent on rebellion, but from a simple lack of maturity in a particular area. In this situation, a simple word of correction will suffice. As Proverbs says, *Foolishness is bound up in the heart of a child; the rod of correction will drive it far from him* (Proverbs 22:15).

The second source of foolishness is the heart of a fool. The only difference between the child and the fool is that the child is correctable and the fool is not. *Though you grind a fool in a mortar with a pestle along with crushed grain, yet his foolishness will not depart from him* (Proverbs 27:22). There is no amount of correction or instruction that can extract the foolishness from the heart of the fool, because the fool is not just ignorant, but intentionally ignorant. The fool embraces the carnal mind as if it were the enlightened mind, and the fool will not relent even when facing the direst of consequences.

The fool is what the Proverbs describe as *stiff-necked*. This image is drawn from the experience of those who worked with oxen to plow fields in ancient Israel. The plowman would follow the ox with a sharp stick called a goad. When he needed the ox to turn, he would prick its neck just enough to indicate that he needed to move in a different direction. Most oxen would respond well to the prodding of the goad, but some oxen would continue to move in the same direction, even after many pricks of the goad. These oxen were called *stiff-necked*. The point is that regardless of how many times you prick a fool in the neck with the goad of instruction, he will not turn from the error of his ways.

At the same time, we must be careful not to label people as fools too quickly. The fact that an individual does not readily accept a word of correction in a moment does not automatically mean he is a fool. There are a number of possible reasons why a word of correction might be rejected, and we must consider them all as possibilities before we make a judgment about the true nature of the person in question.

The first possible reason that a person might not receive a word of correction that I offer them is that I may not have discerned the proper *kairos* (timing) for offering that word. When I offer a word of correction in haste, I inadvertently interrupt the preparatory work of the Spirit of God that is already underway in the heart of the individual in question. Sometimes I offer hasty words of correction simply because I do not trust God to be the one who brings them to repentance, and so I am trying to do it by my own power—which is itself an exercise of the carnal mind. The problem with this strategy is that the carnal mind cannot correct the carnal mind!

Another possibility is that while I have indeed discerned the right time to offer the word of correction, I have not discerned the right way to offer it to this particular person. The prophet Nathan's confrontation of King David in 2 Samuel 12 comes to mind here. Nathan knew that he had to confront the king of Israel, but he also knew he could not simply barge into the presence of the king and level an accusation against him. So he came with a parable that grabbed the heart of the king and stirred up his anger—and then Nathan revealed to the king that he himself was the man in question. The success of Nathan's confrontation of King David was not simply in the fact that he knew when to speak to the king, but that he knew how to speak to him as well.

A third possibility is that while the person's response may give the impression that the word of correction has fallen on deaf ears, it has actually sunk deeply into the heart and is performing a hidden work of transformation there. Sometimes people just don't know how to act in the moment when they are being corrected, yet in the long run we see that the word of correction hit its mark.

Taken together, all of these possibilities lead us to one simple conclusion: we must be patient with people and humble before God. While the carnal mind is God's enemy, not everyone who operates out of it is his enemy. We must be careful not to treat people as enemies of God or as our enemies for that matter. At the end of the day, the mind can only be shepherded when the heart is teachable. While the mind is the lead member of the soul, it can only be accessed by way of the heart. In order to offer correction to the minds of people who may be going astray, you must know how to win their hearts. And demonstrating the possession of patient humility goes a long way toward doing just that.

The key to maintaining a humble heart in this matter is recognizing the carnal tendencies of our own minds. It really is hard to get frustrated with the carnal tendencies of the minds of others when you are fully aware of the carnal tendencies of your own mind. I've often had people who have resisted my correction in the midst of their foolishness come back to me and thank me for my patience after we've come through the ordeal. Whenever that happens, I'm always reminded of the ways in which I've resisted my leaders in seasons past, and I am thankful that they were patient with me.

When we offer patient instruction to those who are operating in the carnal mind, we lead them toward the renewal of the mind. And when we lead the carnal mind into renewal, we transform the whole person and cause him to prove the good, perfect, and acceptable will of God. When the mind is carnal, it is God's enemy, and thus it becomes the instrument of the enemy of our souls. But when the mind is renewed, it comes into agreement with God's thoughts and ways and thus becomes our greatest asset.

6

The New Creation of The Mind

Therefore if anyone is in Christ, he is a new creation.
(2 Corinthians 5:17)

When the mind retreats from the realm of the flesh and returns to the Shepherd and Overseer of the soul, it becomes a spiritual mind. Paul teaches us that the carnal mind is death, but the mind of the Spirit is life and peace (Romans 8:6). This mind of the Spirit is synonymous with the renewed mind that transforms us from within, bringing us into alignment with the good, perfect, and acceptable will of God (Romans 12:2).

Since the mind is the lead member of the soul, wherever it turns, the soul turns in its entirety. The thoughts of the mind influence the emotions of the heart, and the emotions of the heart in turn influence the decisions of the will. When the will is engaged, it exercises the authority to command the body to do its bidding. The behaviors of the body are therefore nothing more than the aftermath of the movements of the soul, which means that if you can move the mind into the Spirit and keep it there, the whole person will live in perfect fellowship with the Spirit of God.

When I speak of the spiritual mind, I am not speaking of the ecstatic mind. When the mind moves out of the flesh and into the Spirit, it simply means that the individual has ceased to entertain the logic of the serpent and has determined to hold to the deep truths of the faith without wavering. Paul tells us that the spiritual mind is simply a mind that has set itself upon the things that the Spirit desires, as opposed to a carnal mind which has set itself upon the things that the flesh desires (Romans 8:5).

The turning of the mind away from the flesh and towards the Spirit is often as simple as the decision to meditate on a verse of Scripture or to turn toward the Lord in a moment of surrendered prayer. The shift from the flesh to the Spirit is typically not very dramatic, and the lack of dramatic experience might cause one to doubt that the shift has actually occurred. But the fact remains that if you have ceased to dwell upon the desires of the flesh and have begun to dwell upon the desires of the Spirit, you have ceased to have the mind of the flesh and have begun to possess the mind of the Spirit.

THE GLORY OF THE SPIRITUAL MIND

While the activities of the spiritual mind may at first

seem to be drab and uninteresting, the character of the spiritual mind itself is preeminently significant. There is nothing more glorious than a renewed mind. In fact, it is the most powerful force in all of creation! So important is the renewed mind that when God set out to renew the fallen creation, he started with the mind.

Think of this: When God created Adam he not only created him perfect, but situated him in a perfect environment. Adam was not capable of struggling in his mind because his external environment perfectly corresponded to his internal nature. Unfortunately, sin changed all of that for us. While eternal salvation has entered the world through the cross of Jesus Christ, the physical world continues to be subject to corruption and decay.

Therefore if anyone is in Christ, he is a new creation; old things have passed away; behold, all things have become new (2 Corinthians 5:17). When Paul says that we have become a new creation in Christ, he is speaking of the new birth experience, which transforms us from the inside out. And the locus of the new creation is not in your physical body, but in your mind. When Paul speaks of being renewed in our minds, he is speaking to the new creation in Christ.

In the original creation God began with the physical world and then put Adam and Eve in it. In the new creation God begins with the new mind, which then becomes the sign of the coming redemption of all things. The new mind is the transformed internal state of the new man who must continue to live in the old world.

God is bringing about a new heaven and a new earth—but he is beginning with a new mind! In the new creation God puts a new man in an old world, a redeemed man in a fallen world. This means that the new Adam must deal with the fact that the external world will not conform to his internal nature. Inwardly, he is being renewed day by day, while outwardly the world is wasting away, and even his physical nature is deteriorating. He must hold to the new creation in his mind and conform his thinking to the new creation even though what he sees in the physical world does not conform to what has happened in his mind.

ADMONITIONS FOR RENEWING THE MIND

The New Testament foresees the struggle that this crisis presents us with and gives us some tools for dealing with it effectively. Romans 12:2 admonishes, *Do not be conformed to the pattern of this age, but be transformed by the renewing of your mind.* We are warned not to be conformed to the pattern of the world because we are under constant pressure to do so. The pattern of this age is a pervasive denial of the new creation. We see appalling situations happening before our very eyes: global warming, world wars, human trafficking, rising divorce rates, economic recessions, etc. Your renewed mind believes that we are quickly approaching the renewal of all things, the new heaven and the new earth, the home of righteousness, but that information is exclusive to the renewed mind. The renewed mind must fight with the eyes and the ears; information gathered from what we see and hear can force the mind into conformity with the cold realities of the present age. The result is that we can become cynical, skeptical, negative, or distrusting —and then we have not simply observed the corruption present in the world through lust, but we have been harmed by it, and may harm others in turn. If we are not vigilant in our thinking, we will begin to conform to the pattern of decay that we see in the physical world. We can thus find ourselves living as though we were still in our sins.

In Philippians 2:5ff Paul gives us this admonition: *Let this mind be in you which was also in Christ Jesus . . .* The spiritual mind and the mind of Christ are synonymous. While the admonition to set the mind upon the things that the Spirit desires can sound abstract and impractical, the admonition to emulate the humility and faith we see exhibited in the life of Jesus is very concrete and practical.

Paul goes on to describe Jesus' way of thinking in this manner: *Who being in very nature God (en morphe theos), considered it not robbery to be equal with God* (Philippians 2:6). The minute we begin to fear that we've lost something, we've lost Jesus' way of thinking. Fear is typically lurking beneath the greatest problems in our thinking. But Jesus had no fear of losing anything, and the sign that he knew he couldn't lose anything was that he willingly emptied himself and gave up everything.

Taking the form (morphe) of a servant (doulos) (Philippians 2:7): here Paul describes the incarnation of Jesus in terms of his willingness to embrace a lower form (the form of a servant) in order to fulfill a higher purpose. The mind of Christ emboldens us to embrace loss as gain, hardship as discipline, testing as patience, knowing that when it looks like we're decreasing we're actually increasing, and as patience has its perfect work we will be perfect, lacking nothing!

Then Paul says that he *humbled himself and became obedient to the point of death* (Philippians 2:8). The death that Paul is urging us to hurry up and die is the death of the flesh. Death for Jesus was an act of obedience, and likewise for us, the death of the flesh is an act of obedience. Just as the Father commanded Jesus to lay down his life and take it up again, we are commanded to repent and be baptized, and when we enter the waters of baptism we go down in the likeness of Christ's death and come up in the likeness of his resurrection. The command to be baptized is not about a water rite but about the command to lay down our lives in solidarity with Christ and take up a new life in solidarity with Christ.

Paul makes this more explicit in Colossians 3:2-3, where he instructs, *Set your minds on things above, where Christ is seated at the right hand of God. For you died and your life is now hidden with Christ in God.* You died to the lower way of thinking and you now live to the higher way of thinking. You died to the decay and deterioration that is in the world, and you are now alive to the power and authority that resides in the heavens at God's right hand. But you must set your mind there in order to live in it.

THE ROLE OF THE PASTORAL

The power of the commands that Paul gives us in regard to the renewal of our minds is only unlocked once these commands are obeyed. There is no human shepherd who can renew our minds for us; only the Spirit of God can renew our minds. That being the case, we might stop here and ask what role the pastoral task plays in the drama of the renewal of the mind.

The idea that a pastor is even necessary presupposes that people can't figure out how to do what Paul has laid out for us. When Paul urges us not to be conformed to the pattern of the world, he gives us a command that flies right over the head of the average believer. When Paul commands us to set our minds on things above where Christ is seated at the right hand of God, he directs us toward a way of living that seems utterly elusive to the average believer. The pastoral task is necessary because the process of renewing the mind is complex.

The Spirit of God is the author of the renewal of the mind; this is certain. However, the pastoral task is necessary because we are not always aware of the degree to which our minds need to be renewed. When we are operating in the carnal mind, we are often unaware of it. In these situations, we need someone we trust to confront us lovingly and direct us toward the truth, so that we can escape the questions, suggestions, and accusations of the enemy that are designed to lead us into temptation.

At this point, many Christians might begin to lament that they have no one they can trust in this way—no church leader who cares enough about them to take the time to shepherd their souls. But this kind of lament smacks of the paralytic at the Pools of Bethesda who complained, *I have no one to help me into the pool* in response to Jesus' offering of healing (John 5:7). The fact of the matter is that if you need an authorized leader of the church to tell you when you are operating in the flesh, then the state of your experience of Christian community is a sad one indeed!

Let the word of Christ dwell in you richly as you teach and admonish one another with all wisdom (Colossians 3:16). Teaching and admonishing one another with all wisdom is supposed to be a core function of Christian community. This means that you shouldn't need an authorized representative of the church to direct you back into the Spirit when you have diverged into the flesh; you should be surrounded by people that you trust to do just that!

The fact that the average church does not function that way is a sign that we have completely misunderstood the role of the authorized representatives of the church. The role of the office-holders in the church is not to do ministry on behalf of the church, but to equip the members of the church to do ministry themselves. This means that the pastoral should beget the pastoral . . . if you have sat under the ministry of an able pastor, you should be continually growing in your ability to function pastorally. Like Abraham and the patriarchs, the body of Christ is supposed to function as a shepherd people . . . but it seems that we would be content to be a shepherded people.

And yet, I must say that even this statement does not communicate the whole truth. In my experience I have discovered that while most believers are quick to say that they desire more interaction with their pastors, the reality is that those same believers have reserved the right to determine the nature of those interactions. Most Christians who say that they desire more interaction with their pastors really mean that they want more of their pastor's time. But the essence of the pastoral is instruction and correction.

The true goal of all pastoral activity is to move the mind and heart out of the flesh and into the Spirit. In order to do this for you, one must intentionally draw attention to the fact that in certain areas of your life your thinking is largely carnal. If you are not willing to allow anyone to shift your thinking from carnality to spirituality, you are not willing to be pastored. And if you are not willing to be pastored, it is no wonder that you have no desire to participate in the great pastoral task of feeding God's sheep and caring for his lambs.

SUBMISSION & AUTHORITY

At the heart of the sad state of the pastoral in contemporary Christianity is a virtually complete disregard for the biblical teaching on authority and submission. This subject is so important that it demands a book of its own, and I hope to take up that task at a later time. But for now it must suffice to acknowledge that from a biblical perspective, the concept of submission is not only the foundation for the pastoral ministry, but is central for understanding the nature of Christian community in general.

In Ephesians 5:21 Paul provides us with a foundational principle for approaching the concept of submission and authority. *Submit to one another out of reverence for Christ*, says the apostle. It is popular these days to preach that we should submit only to Christ and never to one another because we should always reverence Christ and never man. But Paul tells us in this verse that if we truly have reverence for Christ, that reverence will cause us to submit to one another. This also implies that if we do not submit to one another, we ultimately cannot claim to have any reverence for Christ.

From here Paul provides us with six salient examples of what this looks like in different relational contexts. The principle and the examples have a mutually defining effect upon one another; the principle makes it clear that the examples are about how to demonstrate our reverence for Christ through our submission to one another, and the examples make it clear that the command to submit to one another must be followed in a manner appropriate to its relational context. In order to live by this principle, we must discern the appropriate form of submission to offer in every one of our human relationships.

The six examples that Paul proceeds to provide beginning in Ephesians 5:22 can be broken into three sets of twos. The first set relates to the relationship between husband and wife. The wife is to respect her husband in all things and submit to him as unto the Lord and the husband is to love his wife as Christ loved the church and gave himself for her.

It is most common to read this passage and suppose that Paul here calls for the submission of the woman only. But such a reading would do damage to the principle of the previous verse in which Paul commands us to submit to one another. It would not make sense for Paul to command us to submit to one another and then make the wife the sole practitioner of submission in the marriage relationship. It is better to see the honor and respect of the wife toward the husband as the appropriate form of submission that a wife offers her husband and the sacrificial love of the husband for the wife as the appropriate form of reciprocal submission that a husband offers his wife.

If this is not abundantly clear from the first set of examples, it becomes even more clear in the second. Paul begins the 6th chapter of Ephesians with the exhortation, *Children, obey your parents in the Lord, for this is right*. The obedience that a child is to offer his or her parents is the appropriate form that submission takes in this particular relationship. Yet even here the call for reciprocal submission is clearly articulated: *Fathers, do not exasperate your sons, but raise them in the fear and admonition of the Lord* (Ephesians 6:4). While the child offers the parent obedience, the parent offers the child encouragement; both are forms of submission that are appropriate to the specific kind of relationship.

The final set of examples is even more clear than the first two, for here Paul will address the subject of slavery (Ephesians 6:5-9). The apostle begins by exhorting slaves to obey their masters and serve them with sincerity of heart as they would serve Christ. Then Paul exhorts masters to be equitable and fair to their slaves, knowing that they share a common master with them—Christ! So then, the appropriate form of submission that a slave is to offer to a master is service and the appropriate corresponding form of submission that a master is to offer to a slave is fairness.

It is clear that these examples are not exhaustive; there are a host of different kinds of Christian relationships, and within those relationships there are moments that call for different kinds of submission. The key to understanding submission in the body of Christ is that while our submission is offered to one another, our reverence is reserved for Christ. We submit to one another out of reverence for Christ and not out of reverence for one another.

Seeing reverence for Christ as the foundation of Christian submission provides us with the key for discerning the proper form that submission should take in each relational context. If I truly have reverence in my heart for Christ, I will submit myself to Christ as I discern his work in others. Each of the six examples that Paul provides in Ephesians 5:21 - 6:8 resides within the context of an *office*. When I speak of *offices* I am referring to socially recognizable relational occupations, like *father, mother, sister, brother, teacher, student . . .* There is a certain kind of authority that resides within the office of fatherhood and another kind that resides within the office of motherhood, and still another that resides within the office of childhood, etc.

The point of the passage is that in order to demonstrate reverence for Christ in a marriage relationship, the wife must discern the ongoing work of Christ manifested in the office of her husband and the husband must discern the ongoing work of Christ manifested in the office of his wife. Discerning the power of these offices will lead a married couple to always offer these respective forms of submission to one another.

This is true of every other office mentioned in this passage as well, and in fact can be extended to the offices of ministry in the body of Christ. Hebrews 13:17 instructs us to *obey [our] leaders and submit to their authority because they watch over [our] souls as men who must give an account.* Obedience to the leadership of the local church is simply another iteration of the

Pauline principle of submission in Ephesians 5:21. Applying it to our relationships with church leaders requires that we discern the ongoing work of Christ in the offices of leadership appointed by him.

The purpose of this form of submission is to facilitate the task of pastors to watch over our souls. In other words, if we do not submit to them, they are not able to watch over our souls. There is no church leader who has the power to watch over an unsubmitted soul. The unsubmitted soul must simply be released to the chastening of the Lord to have a chance of coming into order and maturity. I would much rather be chastened by the leaders in the body of Christ whom God has set over me than be chastened by the Lord!

However, even in the relationship between church leaders and members there is a reciprocal form of submission which comes into play. Paul gives Timothy some very clear guidelines for relating appropriately to the people of God:

> Do not rebuke an older man, but exhort him as a father, younger men as brothers, older women as mothers, younger women as sisters, with all purity. (1 Timothy 5:1-2)

The principle that Paul is here advancing is that of propriety. Demonstrating propriety in relationships with the people of the church that he leads will require Timothy to rightly discern the ongoing work of Christ within the different groups of people that comprise his congregation. If Timothy is able to discern the character of the ongoing work of Christ within the older men and women and the younger men and women in his congregation, he will continually submit himself to them by exercising temperance and control, by refraining from anger, and by exhibiting patience and respect.

But as mentioned before, the principle of mutual submission applies to all relationships in the body of Christ, not just those already described. Christ reserves the right to speak beyond the borders of typical offices, and when he does so he expects us to discern it and submit to it! Regardless of whether I am an authorized leader of the body of Christ, I am always responsible to discern the appropriate form of submission that I am to offer the believers around me. And I can never become so focused on the offices that I am deaf to the sound of the Lord's voice when he speaks beyond them. When the Lord speaks to me, I must hear it and submit to his voice . . . and if that voice comes to me through the mouth of an eight-year-old child, I am still responsible to hear it and submit to it.

However, though all of this sounds good, applying it is often more difficult than meets the eye. If there were no pride in the body of Christ, this paradigm would be as easy as cake to apply. But pride causes some believers to try to correct or instruct other believers in an improper manner and causes others to reject appropriate correction or instruction from their brothers or sisters. When believers offer instruction and correction out of a prideful spirit it smacks of condescension and judgment, and when believers reject instruction and correction out of a prideful spirit it smacks of insecurity and fear.

The prevalence of pride in the body of Christ is what causes most believers to be wary of the call to participation in the pastoral task. If I offer correction, it not only may be rejected by the proud, but it may cause me to be perceived as proud as well. And since I have the desire neither to contend with the proud nor to be branded as proud myself, it seems that the safest course of action is to refrain from offering any form of correction or instruction to anyone. But the question is, do we value personal safety more than we value the mind of Christ?

THE NEW MIND IS A SIGN

The renewed mind is the sign of the new creation of all things. The creation has yet to be delivered from its bondage to decay, but the renewed mind has already been delivered. Everything else in the world is coming to ruin . . . like the grass that withers and the flower that fades. But the mind of Christ, the spiritual mind, continues to be renewed day by day. Each day those who have embraced the mind of the Spirit are taken deeper into the revelation of the things which God has prepared for those who love him. Each day the heavenly vision becomes more clear. However, the spiritual mind is fragile and its sanctity can be compromised if it is not skillfully led again and again into the presence of the Shepherd and Overseer of our souls.

Will you fight for the mind of Christ? Will you open your eyes to perceive the value of it? The carnal mind is an affront not only to the presence of God but to the identity of the believer! The carnal mind is God's enemy; if I am afraid to call you out of the carnal mind because it might make me your enemy, then I am willing to allow you to remain God's enemy so that you might continue be my friend. Do I care so much about my desire to have a friend that I would allow you to continue to live as God's enemy?

If we would only wake up and recognize the preciousness of the mind of Christ, we would do everything in our power to help one another return to it! We would exhort one another, encourage one another, spur one another on toward love and good works . . . And we would not only seek to give this encouragement to others; we would be quick to receive it–even to seek it–from others as well!

Instead of the *who do you think you are* attitude that most believers have when it comes to receiving correction, the cry of our hearts should be, *Please call me back when I've gone astray! Please don't let me linger long in the flesh! Please, remind me of who I am when I've lost my mind!*

7

The Way of the Heart

Guard your heart, for it is the
well spring of life.
(Proverbs 4:23)

When we are talking about the heart, we are speaking of the Hebraic concept of the command center, or seat of the emotions. Emotions are very powerful things, but we must emphasize that they are always the product of thoughts. In fact, it is very easy to confuse thoughts and feelings. If someone says, *I feel like you don't like me*, that person has confused a thought with a feeling. *You don't like me* is an idea, not a feeling. The feeling that comes from that idea, or thought, is *rejection*. When you feel like someone doesn't like you, what has actually happened is that since you thought (or believed) that person didn't like you, you began to experience the emotion we call rejection.

The problem with feelings is that they are not always accurate. They are based upon thoughts, but not developed thoughts—they are the reflexive response to micro-interpretive thoughts. Your mind is constantly assessing, evaluating, and interpreting everything that you experience; your heart is constantly responding to what the mind gives it by producing emotional responses; these emotions then give the will an indication of how to respond to any given situation. This is why we often feel things that we later discover to be completely unrelated to reality. You experience terror when you hear a noise —only to realize that it was just a friend playing a prank on you. Your mind interpreted the sound as dangerous or violent, but the interpretation was incorrect. Your friend's true desire was to be funny, not to harm you.

THE HEART IN THE BIBLE

In the Bible, the emotions are defined as the *heart*. The term *heart* appears in Scripture over 700 times! Compare this with only about 150 occurrences of the word *mind*. In the New Testament the heart is spoken of 156 times, compared 74 mentions of the mind. At first glance it could be argued that from a biblical perspective the heart is far more important than the mind. I think a better explanation is that the heart is where all that happens in the mind manifests, and so to get to the mind you have to deal with what's in the heart.

The heart is important because it is the place where

understanding takes place; nine times the heart is associated with understanding in the New Testament. Here are a few examples:

For this people's heart has grown dull, and with their ears they can barely hear, and their eyes they have closed, lest they should see with their eyes and hear with their ears and understand with their heart and turn, and I would heal them. (Matthew 13:15)

When anyone hears the word of the kingdom and does not understand it, the evil one comes and snatches away what has been sown in his heart. This is what was sown along the path. (Matthew 13:19)

And Jesus, aware of this, said to them, "Why are you discussing the fact that you have no bread? Do you not yet perceive or understand? Are your hearts hardened? (Mark 8:17)

They are darkened in their understanding, alienated from the life of God because of the ignorance that is in them, due to their hardness of heart. (Ephesians 4:18)

My purpose is that they may be encouraged in heart and united in love so that they may have the full riches of complete understanding in order that they may know the mystery of God, namely Christ. (Colossians 2:2)

When the heart is hardened, understanding is impossible. When the heart is encouraged, the full riches of complete understanding are available. One of the things that's been so frustrating to me over the years is speaking things that are simple, easy to understand, straightforward, and easily applicable, and in response hearing people say things like, *I don't understand* or *That doesn't make sense to me.* For years I thought I just needed to learn how to communicate better. But then I discovered from these verses that understanding cannot possibly transpire in a hardened heart.

This is significant! If understanding happens in the heart, then reasoning with someone's mind to get him to understand and/or agree with what you're saying is futile. You can't convince the mind when the heart has hardened against understanding. A hardened heart is at the root of every relational problem. This explains why Jesus said that Moses gave the provision of divorce because of the hardness of hearts. Every marital problem, every ministry problem, every church split—every broken relationship has at least a couple of hardened hearts to thank for it.

So often we try to solve problems by addressing the key issues, and this is important. But the root is not the issue; the root is the heart, and therefore you cannot get to the heart of an issue until you get to the heart of the heart itself. This means that the task of shepherding the heart is really about softening it, or as Paul says in Colossians 2:2, encouraging it. When the heart is encouraged it opens up to receive the full riches of complete understanding.

This also gives us a clue as to the real problem behind a

hardened heart: discouragement. Discouragement is the heart's most formidable impediment to understanding. It causes the heart to shut down, to close up on itself and allow nothing else in. It imprisons the heart in its own pain and holds it there without bail. The shepherd must be skilled in the ministry of encouragement in order to set the heart free from its prison of discouragement.

When the heart is hardened, not only is understanding impossible, but so is faith. A hardened heart cannot believe, so it cannot please God. In fact, a hardened heart militates toward unbelief and ultimately turns from the living God. This is why Scripture refers to the hardened heart as wicked.

What we need are more shepherds like Barnabas, whose Hebrew name meant *son of encouragement*. Barnabas came alongside people and led them from one place to another. He brought Paul out of obscurity and into fellowship with the Jerusalem church. He brought great encouragement to the young church at Antioch. He brought Paul up from Tarsus and established him in ministry in Antioch. And he brought John Mark into the apostolic mission to the Gentiles.

Barnabas was able to lead people forward in their walk with Christ because he was skillful in the ministry of encouragement. Encouragement is the key to shepherding of heart, not reason. The heart does not respond to reason even though it is the seat of the understanding. It only understands when it is encouraged. This means that the gift of encouragement is the most powerful gift a shepherd can have. When it is exercised, it has the power to soften hardened hearts and open them up to understanding.

JESUS & THE WOMAN AT THE WELL

When Jesus had his encounter with the woman at the well (John 4), he did not try to convince her that he was the Messiah or confront her with the evil of her ways. Instead, he first asked her for a drink of water. This was a huge step because she was the town outcast. She was drawing water at 3 pm, rather than early in the morning with the other women. The other women spurned her presence because of her lifestyle. In addition to this potential reason for avoiding her, at that time Jewish men did not speak to women in public at all, and no Jew would ever speak to a Samaritan in public. Jesus, however, didn't seem to be bothered by her lifestyle, her gender, or her ethnicity. He was not only willing to speak to her, but to request and receive water from her as well.

The willingness of Jesus to be served by this woman was a powerful statement of the posture of his heart toward her. This was amazing to her and it encouraged her greatly. It caused her heart to perk up from the place where it had been buried under an avalanche of rejection, and then she was ready to be set free.

How is it that you, a Jew, can ask me, a Samaritan, for something to drink? she asked. Translation: Why are you so uninhibited by the things that inhibit everyone else? Jesus here demonstrated a freedom that no one else demonstrated, and that freedom allowed him to touch this woman's heart in a place she had never been touched before by a man. In fact, it was significant that Jesus was a man, because men were her problem. She couldn't get it right with men; now a man was going to make it right for her!

Jesus responded, *If you knew the gift of God and who it was that asked you for a drink, you'd ask him and he'd give you living water so that you'd never thirst again.* This was the offer of grace and he articulated it in terms that related to her present location: just as he and the woman were standing before a well that gives us water, he points out that she was now standing before a well that gave living water, and he was that well.

Before confronting her problem, Jesus opened her eyes to who he was and to the availability of grace that came with his presence. She had no idea to whom she was speaking, and consequently was completely ignorant of the gift of God. That's why she was in her situation. We must recognize that when we are ministering to someone whose heart has hardened around hurt, pain, rejection, abandonment, etc., we are dealing with someone who doesn't know the gift of God and is unaware of how available it is. With the Samaritan woman, Jesus used the analogy of the well to open her eyes to the offer of grace that came with his loving presence.

However, at first she didn't understand the analogy because she was stuck in the natural, the soul, and thought only in terms of natural things. *You have nothing to draw with and the well is deep*, she replied. She heard him say living water, but she was still thinking in terms of natural water. *Are you greater than our father Jacob, who dug this well and drank from it himself?* Jesus responded, *Everyone who drinks this water will thirst again, but anyone who drinks my water will never thirst again, but that water will become a well that springs up into everlasting life.*

Suddenly she realized that Jesus as speaking of more than mere physical water, yet she remained unable to perceive his offer as anything other than an answer to her situational need: *Sir, give me this water so that I don't have to come to this well anymore.* The well was a place of shame for her. She could feel the eyes of the townspeople on her when she came in the afternoon to draw water. If there was any chance that she could escape their stares and still have water, she would take it!

Although she still misunderstood what Jesus was offering, at this point she asked for the water. Asking is a sign that the heart is open to receive. It doesn't mean that the problem is solved, but that the heart is willing to receive whatever medicine is necessary to cure it of its infirmity. This is the place where correction or confrontation will actually do some good. And so Jesus used the occasion of the openness of her heart to confront the issue of her lifestyle.

Go get your husband, Jesus replied. This was the sore spot she was hoping not to have to face. This was the source of all the shame she had carried for years. The fact that Jesus now brought this subject to the foreground was terrifying for her.

I have no husband, she responded, hoping not to have to explain the complexity of her situation. Then Jesus demonstrated that he had no need of an explanation; in fact, he had come to explain her situation to her! *Indeed*, said Jesus, *you have had five, and the man you now have won't even give you his name; the best he gives you is his bed. So you are right when you say that you have no husband!* (my paraphrase)

This was confrontation at its best! Jesus would not allow her to hide. He wouldn't allow her to escape the issue. He put it right in her face—but not until he had given her the promise of grace and of eternal life. He made sure that her heart was encouraged enough to open up, and only then did he confront her.

So often we harm people because we confront them too early, without the right amount of encouragement, and we wonder why their hearts shut down even further. We wonder why they don't see what to us is so obvious. But we haven't properly diagnosed the problem; the heart has hardened around pain, around hurt, around rejection, around abandonment. Sin is only a byproduct of that hardening; sin is only possible when the heart has become hard.

Jesus always did something to soften the hearts of sinners before commanding them to go and sin no more. Either he healed them physically, or sent away their accusers, or spoke to them when no one else would, or fed them miraculously . .

there was always a demonstration of divine grace designed to soften the heart with encouragement and open it up to the full riches of complete understanding. Then and only then would he bring the direct confrontation of sin and command repentance.

We must learn to offer people grace before we get in their face. We must learn to encourage before we confront. And we must learn that encouragement is far more than simple care. Encouragement does not simply come through empathy. Empathy is a way of saying, *I am with you.* Encouragement says, *I have something that you don't have, and I'm offering it to you now.* Through empathy you offer to sit with someone in a dark place, but through encouragement you lift him out of the darkness.

If we are going to effectively shepherd the soul, we must learn the ministry of encouragement, and learn it well. Then and only then will we have the power to lead people to green pastures where they can safely graze and find rest. This ministry of encouragement will be the subject of our next chapter.

8

The Ministry of Encouragement

The Sovereign Lord has given me a well-instructed tongue,
to know the word that sustains the weary.
(Isaiah 50:4)

During the last days of my grandmother's life, we were all praying for her to go home and be with the Lord, rather than linger on in her condition of suffering. After several days of this, my good friend came to me and said, *I prayed for you and the Lord showed me that he loves you so much that he won't take your grandmother until you fully release her in your heart.* This didn't encourage me; it made me angry because it suggested to me that God was cruel for letting my grandmother suffer until I figured out how to release her from my heart.

On another occasion we had a couple in our church who lost their baby boy when he was only ten days old. We were all devastated for them and with them, and everyone just wanted to find a way to encourage and support them. But one well-meaning but ill-mannered individual took it upon himself to prophesy to the couple that the Lord said not to worry because he was going to give them another son. When I discovered this, I was furious. The last thing this couple needed two days after losing their first son was a prophecy about the birth of their second. Both of these examples were attempts at encouragement which were not encouraging in the least bit.

Virtually every member of the body of Christ desires to be encouraging, but it seems that very few actually possess the wisdom and skill to be a consistent source of encouragement. When most Christians realize they lack the wisdom to know what to say in a particular situation, they at least have the wisdom to say nothing. But maturity demands that we grow beyond the say-nothing stage. Maturity demands that we learn to discern what to say and how to say it in order to become the kind of encouragers we long to become.

And so we see that the ability to encourage necessitates the possession of wisdom. In order to rightly and consistently encourage one another, we need God to give us the kind of wisdom spoken of by the prophet Isaiah:

> *The Sovereign Lord has given me a well-instructed tongue, to know the word that sustains the weary. He wakens me morning by morning, wakens my ear to listen like one being instructed.* (Isaiah 50:4)

We must ask the Lord to give instruction to our tongues so that we might know what to say and what not to say, and we must ask for this wisdom on a daily basis. This type of wisdom does not come from reading books or taking classes. God must give it to you, and he will if you ask him for it and believe that you have received it every day!

But Paul's letter to Titus contains an exhortation regarding encouragement which might seem very peculiar at first glance. For here Paul exhorts Titus to *encourage and rebuke with all authority* (Titus 2:15). It takes authority to rebuke; this we know and understand. But the idea that it takes just as much authority to encourage people as it does to rebuke them is not a common notion. The implication of Paul's admonition here is that just as a rebuke would fall flat if not communicated in an authoritative way, so a word of encouragement communicated in the absence of authority will ultimately fall flat as well.

The pastoral task demands that you lay hold of the authority to encourage. This does not require a seminary degree or an official ordination. Authority is the incorporation of faith and confidence. It begins with faith because it is dependent upon the clear and present work of the Spirit of God in your life, and it is completed by confidence because it requires you to unashamedly invite your brother or sister to become a full participant in that work of the Spirit.

Authoritative encouragement is more than friendly encouragement; there is an element of command in it. Be encouraged! It's a command. God practiced authoritative encouragement with Joshua when he commanded him to *be strong and take courage* (Joshua 1:7, 9, 18). Authoritative encouragement is God's command through another human vessel.

Authoritative encouragement is inherently prophetic as well: *Arise, shine, for your light has come* (Isaiah 60:1). The command to arise and shine is not arbitrary, but is based upon the prophetic discernment that *your light has come*. Sometimes the reason our words of encouragement fall to the ground is because we are commanding people to rise and shine even though we have not seen by the Spirit that their light has come!

THE THREE TENSES OF ENCOURAGEMENT

God reveals himself to us as the God who was, who is, and who is to come. To know him as the God who was means to have intimate knowledge of what he has done. To know him as the God who is means to have intimate knowledge of what he is doing. To know him as the God who is to come means to have intimate knowledge of what he is about to do. In like manner, encouragement can also manifest either as a reminder of what God has done, an awakening to what God is doing, or an announcement of what God is about to do. The "past tense" form of encouragement requires the memory. The "present tense" form requires discernment. The "future tense" form requires revelation.

The past tense form of encouragement cannot be underestimated. Discouragement is typically a powerful form of amnesia: we so easily forget what God has done, and when we forget what God has done for us, we tend to become acutely aware of what the devil is doing to us. We tend to think that what God does for us is temporary, that we can lose it or mess it up . . . and because we believe in the transience of God's works, we experience them as transient realities—it will be to us according to our faith. The pastoral task begins with the resolve to believe in the ongoing validity of the work of the Lord on behalf of others: if Jesus does something in someone's life, we must make up our minds that we are going to believe in it. This is the posture we must maintain toward our fellow believers in Christ.

Encouragement is the act of reminding a person of what God has done, how powerful it was, and of the permanence of the works of the Lord. Jesus died once for all, and he does not need to die again! He was raised from the dead once, and he does not need to arise again! When he delivers you, he delivers you once, and he does not need to deliver you again! The power of the past tense form of encouragement is that it continues to affirm the ongoing validity of what God has done in the past in the face of evidence to the contrary.

The present tense form of encouragement is just as powerful, but it takes more than memory: it takes discernment to become consciously aware of what God is doing right now. What is God doing? What is God saying? Typically, discouragement comes as a demonic response to some divine work. When God is on the move in a person's life, so is Satan. Encouragement takes place as we refuse to speak in agreement with what Satan is doing in someone's life and we resolve to speak in agreement with what God is doing.

While the past tense form of encouragement takes only intimate knowledge of a person's historic walk with God, in order to exercise the present tense form of encouragement we need discernment. Discernment is the ability to see. It is the ability to stand in the light when everyone is in the darkness of discouragement, to see through the darkness in order to bring someone else into the light. This ability can't simply be learned in a book. It can't be taught, it must be "caught," as it were, through prayer. Yet it is a non-negotiable spiritual skill that every effective minister must learn.

Back in 2005 my wife and I were holding early morning prayer meetings in our apartment in Emeryville and a handful of people were coming. One morning my friend from SoCal was in town and wanted to join us. That morning in the middle of the prayer meeting I looked up and saw an angel standing at the corner of my coffee table. He was brilliant, gleaming, powerful!

After the prayer meeting was over my friend came to me and said, *Did you see that angel at the corner of your coffee table?* He had seen the same angel in the same spot at the same time I had. That's pretty powerful, wouldn't you say? Yet despite this, a few days later I was so discouraged about how certain things were going with the church that I called the same friend and just began to pour out my heart. When I finished he asked me a simple question that led to a simple conclusion: *Don't you remember that an angel stood in your living room a couple days ago? Now I'm no biblical scholar, but it seems to me that God doesn't just send angels for no reason. If God sent an angel to you, it means that something is happening on your behalf in the heavenlies!*

What he said to me was incredibly encouraging because it reminded me of what God was doing in my life. I was discouraged because I couldn't see what God was doing at that moment, and all I could see were my problems. When he encouraged me he didn't try to get me to look on the bright side or to see the glass as half full. He simply pointed to a completely transcendent reality: that what God was doing on my behalf in the unseen was much more powerful than what the enemy was doing to hinder me in the seen.

Isn't this what happened with Elisha and his servant when the army surrounded the city and his servant was freaking out? Elisha was calm because he could see what God was doing, and therefore he was not moved by what he saw in the natural. He was not discouraged in the face of his obstacle because he saw that which was invisible. Then he prayed for his servant: *Lord, open his eyes so that he may see!* (2 Kings 6:17) This is the prayer behind the present tense form of encouragement: *Lord, open our eyes that we may see!*

If we are discouraged, it simply means we have forgotten

what God is doing in our lives. Through the ministry of encouragement we are able to call one another back to the place of acknowledgement of the present work of God. My spiritual father does this for me all the time, and it is one of the most powerful ways of escape from the jaws of discouragement. He simply reminds me of what I myself have reported from the Lord and of what I myself have testified to seeing God do on my behalf. On many occasions this is all that is needed in order to lead me back into the presence of the Shepherd and Overseer of our souls.

The third form of encouragement, what I call the future tense form of encouragement, takes us into the realm of prophecy. Authoritative encouragement is prophetic at its core because it is never just a command, but comes with a promise. God's commands are always based upon his promises, so we must see to it that our commands are based upon promises from God as well. The prophetic promise is the foundation of the authoritative command. Without a prophetic promise, it is almost impossible to issue an authoritative command.

The most powerful form of encouragement you can give a person is this prophetic, future tense form of encouragement. When you speak over a person and tell her what is to come when she is in the throes of despair, that prophetic word has the power to lift her up to see God's perspective on her current situation. Prophetic insight changes everything! With it you have authority to command encouragement, because you know what God is doing and is getting ready to do tomorrow at about this time. It is our right as sons and daughters of God to know things that are to come, to speak them before they come to pass, and to declare things that are not as though they were!

Once again, however, this level of encouragement is not learned in a book; it cannot be taught, but must be sought, and then caught. We should be crying out to God day and night that he would give us the Spirit of wisdom and revelation in the knowledge of him so that the eyes of our understanding would be enlightened! We need to cry out to God day and night that he would open our eyes and open our ears and open our mouths that we might speak words of heaven and not of the earth!

THE DISCOURAGED PERSPECTIVE

What makes all of this possible is determining in our hearts not to moved by the perspective of the discouraged. When people are discouraged, their perspective is skewed. If we are persuaded by that skewed perspective, we find ourselves in just as much bondage as they are. What is important to note here is that while we are supposed to empathize with people, we are not supposed to share their discouragement. The prophet Isaiah said of Christ that he would not lose heart until he brought justice to the nations. You and I must also enter into that Messianic ministry of encouragement which empowers us not to lose heart in the face of disheartening circumstances.

All of this means that the pastoral task begins in our own

hearts; it begins when we refuse to succumb to discouragement, when we resolve to treat discouragement like we treat the devil. We cannot yield to it, even for a moment! It is as wicked as lust and fornication. Paul said to flee fornication, and we must also flee discouragement! It causes our hearts to harden, it darkens our understanding, it alienates us from the life of God and leaves us stranded in utter ignorance. It snuffs out our light and hides it under a bowl. When we allow ourselves to be discouraged we come into the darkness, into the place where we can no longer see what God is doing, and John said that it is only if we walk in the light as Jesus is in the light that we can truly have fellowship with one another.

If we fellowship in the darkness, we can only experience the fellowship of darkness. If we work from the place of darkness, we can only bring about the fruitless deeds of darkness that Paul commanded us to have nothing to do with (Ephesians 5:11). But if we walk in the light as Christ is in the light, we have fellowship with one another and the blood of Jesus Christ purifies us from all sin (1 John 1:7).

This is how we effectively shepherd the heart: we encourage it. When we have encouraged the heart, it opens up to the full riches of complete understanding. It is brought out of its place of ignorance and into the knowledge of God. It is reconnected to the life of God, and it begins to rejoice in the Lord and make its boast in him. That's how powerful a little bit of encouragement can be; it can change someone's life forever!

But encouraging the heart requires the discernment of just the right word—*the word that sustains the weary*, as mentioned above. For each weary person this is a right word that has the power to sustain her, and our ability to encourage is dependent upon our ability to discern that right word. While this task may seem daunting, the key to cultivating the knowledge of the word that sustains the weary is the declaration of faith.

The declaration of faith: each morning when you arise, begin by declaring Isaiah 50:4 before the Lord. *Lord, I thank you that you have given me an instructed tongue and today I will know how to speak a word in season to him who is weary. You awaken me morning by morning; you awaken my ear to listen as one being instructed!*

Rather than beginning your day with discouragement and anxiety, begin with confidence and assurance. *Because the Lord has instructed my tongue, I have an anointing to speak to whomever I encounter today.* You've got to begin by believing and declaring this even if you don't feel it so that you are careful not to disqualify yourself because of what you feel.

The prophet goes on to say,

> *The Lord God has opened my ear; and I was not rebellious, nor did I turn away. I gave my back to those who struck me, and my cheeks to those who plucked out the beard; I did not hide my face from shame and spitting.* (Isaiah 50:4)

Here the prophet is describing the ministry of the coming

Messiah as one with open ears and an instructed tongue; he knows how to receive the words of the Father, and he knows how to give them to the right people and at the right time. And he was not rebellious. This means that when he received the words of the Father, he received the command to give them to his people, and he did not rebel against that command. Even when he knew that what he said would be rejected, he determined that he would not be rebellious, but would speak the words the Father gave him to speak.

The prophet foretells that the Messiah would suffer the ultimate rejection for the words he spoke. He would speak words of encouragement, and in return men would strike his back, pluck out his beard, and spit on him. Yet even knowing that this level of rejection awaited him, the Messiah determined that he would open his ear and not be rebellious—he would not restrain the words of the Father in order to protect himself from rejection.

So many of us get this all wrong in the contemporary church. We tend to speak out when the Father has not given it to us to speak, and we refrain from speaking when the Father is giving it to us to speak. We need the Spirit of the Lord to rest upon us again, the Spirit of wisdom and understanding, the Spirit of counsel and might, the Spirit of knowledge and of the fear of the Lord!

What is the word that we are not to refrain from speaking? The word that sustains the weary! The word in season that sustains the weary is not a verbal assault on the sins of our age, but a verbal proclamation of the good news for those who are weary. The prophet says of the Messiah that he will not hesitate to risk everything to pull someone out of a pit. He will risk rejection, persecution, and even death to speak a word in season to him who is weary.

The ministry of authoritative encouragement begins not when the people you minister to affirm it in you and submit to it, but when you receive it from God and submit to it. No one else will see it if you don't. No one else will believe it if you don't. No one else will receive it if you don't. From this day forward, I declare that you will trust and not be ashamed! You're going to speak the words of the Lord, and he's going to work on your behalf!

So we have seen that the task of shepherding the soul requires skill in dealing with the mind and heart. In our next chapter, we will move on to the will. The will is what actually changes the material realm. It is a leader, and so to effectively pastor it we must make it a follower without breaking it. In fact, we will see that shepherding the will is not about weakening it in order to bring it into submission, but about strengthening it in order to bring it into conformity with the will of God. This is the subject of our next chapter.

9

The Will & the Crisis of Integrity

A double-minded man is unstable in all his ways.
(James 1:8)

While the emotions are primarily passive, the will is active. Willing is what you do, not what happens to you. If you are looking at the menu of your favorite restaurant and you can't decide what to eat, you are trying to determine what you want so that you can will it by placing your order. If your appetite is not giving you any useful information, you simply make a decree by the power of your will: *I'll have the salmon!*

There's an almost infinitely powerful quality to the human will. Each generation of human accomplishments causes the accomplishments of the previous generation to pale in comparison. One hundred years ago our forebears would not have believed that it was possible to build a craft that could take you from San Francisco to London in twelve hours! Or how about the mobile phone? Many of us can look back to a period in our not-too-distant past when we wouldn't have believed it was possible to create a pocket-sized device with which we could make phone calls, send emails, surf websites, send and receive money, store hundreds of contacts, schedule events for years to come, and get instant turn-by-turn directions to virtually any location on the planet. Yet today these abilities are so common that we can't even imagine living without them.

All of this is attributable to the human will. The human will focuses its attention in one direction, and cities somehow spring up out of the ground. It focuses its attention in another direction and cures for diseases are discovered. The human will possesses the potential to solve an amazingly complex constellation of problems, and we have yet to discover its limitations.

At the same time, the will is also capable of a host of epoch-altering atrocities. It can start wars and end millions of lives. It can create weapons of mass destruction that threaten the very existence of our planetary life. It can create diseases which have the power to extinguish humanity, and it can divide the world into categories of existence so that in one part of the world there is wealth and opulence and in another there is starvation and oppression.

The will is the easiest member of the soul to understand because it is the most straightforward. The will manifests itself concretely in the actions of the body. If you slap someone, you have simply exercised your will in the direction of that person's face. Everything you do is a manifestation of your will, so the will is clearly seen through the actions of the body.

This objective quality of the will makes it not only easy to study, but the focal point of most discipleship processes. Discipleship, in many sectors of contemporary Christianity, is the training of the will; its outcome is the shaping of behavior. From this perspective, discipleship is about Christian truth manifested by Christian discipline and Christian ethics. In other words, discipleship typically has the threefold objective of teaching young believers what to think about God, how to grow in relationship with him through the Word, worship, and fellowship, and how to act in the world.

The problem I find is that the gap between theology, spirituality, and ethics is not properly bridged in this schema. How many people have you known who appeared to be fervently on fire for the Lord as long as they were engaged in a particular program, but ended up falling into the trap of the enemy when their context changed? I've seen this happen again and again and it never ceases to amaze me. The church is filled with people who appear to be spiritually mature when their activities are observed within the life of the church. But the reality is that these people are not always as mature as they seem.

Many believers who appear to be mature in the Lord have actually matured within the system of the local church, rather than in the Lord. Discipleship programs tend to set out certain volitional requirements: *To remain in this program you must do this and this and this, and you must refrain from doing this and this and this.* The people who learn to conform their wills to the requirements of the program may appear spiritually mature, but all they've proven is that they can conform to a program while they're in it. The test of spiritual maturity is not what you do within a structure, but what you do when there is no structure.

How much of your spiritual life is really yours and how much is merely mandated? Whatever is yours apart from any mandate, that is the substance of your spiritual life. If you pray ten hours a day while you're in the program but pray ten minutes a day after the program is over, you really only have a ten-minute-a-day spirituality. The exercise of praying ten hours a day in the program did not flow from your will to *be*, but from your will to *conform*.

THE TWOFOLD CRISIS

When the will is shepherded, it begins to make different decisions apart from any sense of obligation. The shepherded will needs no legislation; it wills what it wills because it wills, not because it must. The objective of the shepherding of the will is to teach people to will of their own accord what is in accord with the will of God. And when we think of it this way, we begin to realize that dealing with the will is not as straightforward as we might have thought.

The difficulty in shepherding the will is due to a *crisis of interpretation* and a *crisis of source*. The will is best understood as the purpose or intent behind each and every action. It is possible for your action to communicate something foreign to your intent. This means that, although every action is connected to the will, actions must be carefully interpreted before an evaluation of the will is made.

Here is an example: I once flew to Phoenix and brought my golf clubs with me in a hard black travel case. When I got to the baggage claim in Phoenix, I saw an older man rolling my golf clubs away. I approached him and said, *Excuse me, sir, but those happen to be my clubs.* He looked at me sternly and said, *No, these are my clubs!*

Well, let's check the name tag to be sure, I replied . . . and sure enough, the clubs were mine. The man looked back at the baggage claim area and saw another golf travel case, and realized that he had inadvertently taken my clubs. What the man had been about to do was steal my clubs: that was the reality. In another moment or two my clubs would have been gone. However, stealing was not his intent. He simply wanted to play some golf and failed to anticipate the possibility that someone else might have a golf case identical to his.

The pastoral task gets tricky when you are trying to discover the intent behind the actions of an individual. *Why did you do that? What was your motive, the driving force behind your decision? What was your intent? What did you hope to get out of that?* The pastor is here at the mercy of the sheep in a sense; if the sheep refuse to be honest with themselves and with their pastor, they may deny anything that reflects poorly upon their internal world. The flesh equips the soul with a self-justifying mechanism that is designed to prevent it from being faced with the need to change. It provides the mind with the necessary rationale for making sinful actions look justifiable, understandable, and even unavoidable.

This is the crisis of interpretation: how do I interpret the will behind the actions of the people I am responsible for? There are two extremes: either I'll let them off the hook too easily and never require them to change, or I'll judge them too severely, over-interpreting their every action and unearthing sinful intent from under every stone.

The crisis of source refers to the fact that the will is not an independent entity; the content of the will is always based upon what the mind believes and what the heart feels. Our thoughts and feelings are the sources of the decisions of our will. The problem is that when the mind and heart believe contradictory things, the will contradicts itself as well. At times I may believe that my wife loves me, but at other times I may believe that she doesn't love me. At times I may believe that God's plan for my life is the best for me, but at other times I may believe he's just using me and doesn't really care about me. At times I may believe that my life is a good thing, but at other times I may feel worthless, useless, and weary of it. What I don't anticipate is that if I believe two antithetical things, I will inadvertently *will* two antithetical things and there will be a split in my behavior patterns.

When the will is split, the human person experiences something akin to a dissociative identity disorder. How is it that I am one person in certain contexts and another person in another context? How is it that in one context I want only to worship the Lord, but in another context I intensely want things that I should not be wanting, and I find myself doing things that I should not be doing? This is the crux of the matter when it comes to shepherding the will. While the manifestation of the will is straightforward, the origins of and reasons behind the will are often exceedingly obscure.

PURSUING ONENESS OF SELF

The task of shepherding the will is best understood as a process of integration: that is, integrity is the goal. The term *integrity* conveys a sense of oneness of self. Integrity is defined as *the state of being whole or undivided*. To have integrity is to have wholeness: literally, to be one person.

Human beings are notoriously duplicitous; we think one way, speak one way, and act another way. Have you ever known anyone who was usually late, yet always intended to be on time? That type of person thinks and speaks like a timely person but acts like a tardy person. This demonstrates a lack of integrity between his thinking and his acting: that is, he is fundamentally divided.

A biblical example is found in James 1:5–8:

If any of you lacks wisdom, he should ask God, who gives generously to all without finding fault, and it will be given to him. But when he asks, he must believe and not doubt, because he who doubts is like a wave of the sea, blown and tossed by the wind. That man should not think he will receive anything from the Lord; he is a double-minded man, unstable in all he does.

The double-minded man is the man who lacks integrity: he is simultaneously a person of great faith and a person of great unbelief. This duplicity creates instability and insecurity. You never know whether this person is going to become stronger in the face of adversity, or fall by the wayside. A person of integrity, on the other hand, is a person who has achieved oneness of self through the full integration of his thoughts, words, and actions. If you were to look into this person's mind you would see exactly what comes out of her mouth, and if you lined up her words with her actions they would match perfectly.

There has only been one man in history who modeled this perfectly, and his name is Jesus. But there have been many who through the process of being conformed to his image have demonstrated a high degree of integrity.

Integrity, as the state of oneness of self, is the prerequisite for possessing self-confidence, self-acceptance, and self-love. The self-divided man cannot be self-confident because he doesn't know which self to be confident in. Can I be confident in my words when they do not agree with my thoughts (when, for instance, I say nice things to someone I don't like)? Can I be confident in my actions when they do not agree with my words? Which self do I accept: my thinking self, my speaking self, or my acting self? I can only accept myself, be confident in myself, and love myself when I have become one self.

One thing I have desired of the Lord; that will I seek, says the psalmist (Psalm 27:4). *I do not count myself to have apprehended, but one thing I do*, says the apostle Paul (Philippians 3:13). In order for the soul to be perfected in grace, the mind must find its one thing, its center. Only then can the will be centered as well.

The pastoral process should focus on teaching people how to take every thought captive to the obedience of Christ, rather than upon breaking the human will by harsh criticism. Criticism does not empower the will, it disempowers it. The will only works properly when it is empowered, and since the will reflects the thoughts and the emotions, the mind and emotions must be empowered in order for the will to be empowered.

Sin is not the weakness of the will, but the power of the will pointed in the wrong direction. The goal is to point it in the right direction by giving people the power to take authority over their thinking. Behind every decision is a belief. In order for people to make better decisions, they must form better beliefs. The will is simply the enforcer of the belief system.

In order to set people free from a sinful behavior, you must move their minds out of deception and into the truth. Knowing the truth sets us free. Bondage always comes from the lie. The will is not set free when it is commanded directly, but when the mind is commanded to repent and believe.

The psalmist says of God, *He restores my soul* (Psalm 23:3). The word *restore* comes from the Hebrew *shuv,* which means *to turn or to repent. He turns my soul,* says the psalmist. He turns it away from the path of error and toward the path of truth. And he is able to turn our souls because he is our shepherd, our pastor. The pastoral task is to turn the soul, and this task is accomplished by causing the mind to believe and by turning it away from the path of unbelief and the realm of the flesh.

But as we will see in the next and final chapter, the most powerful form of the shepherding of the soul does not take the form of authoritative command, but of compelling example. In this next chapter we will take a deep look into the pastoral methodology of Jesus in order to discover the ultimate secret behind his ability to effectively shepherd the souls of his twelve disciples. To this subject we now turn.

10

The Values of the Shepherd

*Lord, teach us to pray, as John also
taught his disciples.*

(Luke 11:1)

Jesus was the least religious religious leader in the history of religious leaders. At first blush he might seem typical: he appears on the scene as a Jewish rabbi, a role that was central to the Judaism of the first century. He is a Jew among Jews, and he engages in the religious life of the Jewish people as a full participant. When he invites those who would become his disciples to come and follow him, he does so in a manner that is familiar to them. In Israel then, when a rabbi invited you to become his disciple, he was inviting you into a lifelong process of conforming your mind and heart to his teaching so that your life might fully exemplify it. This is why the disciples had to leave their boats (which represented their former way of life) and their fathers (who represented their prior system of influences) in order to answer the call. The call was not so much an opportunity to hang out with Jesus, but to become like Jesus in every way.

THE UNIQUENESS OF JESUS

However, the way Jesus operated within this religious milieu was completely unique. Instead of testing those who desired to become his disciples in order to assess their aptitude, he simply chose whom he wanted, with no apparent regard for their ability either to understand or to exemplify his teaching. Jesus not only called, but he took responsibility for the outcome of that call. When Peter, for instance, felt inadequate in the face of that call and bade him depart, Jesus calmed his fears with the promise, *Don't be afraid; from now on you will catch men* . . . (Luke 5:10)

The disciples of Jesus don't have to make themselves; Jesus will make them. They don't have to change their own lives; Jesus will change their lives. All they have to do is make the decision to forsake all and follow Jesus. And this one requirement–as we all know from personal experience–is not an easy one. Walking away from their boats and nets was easy; walking away from their personal agendas and future aspirations was a much longer process, and it took Jesus three years to get them to the place where they were ready and willing to fully surrender their lives to him. It was at this point that they became his witnesses, which was what he promised from the beginning: that they would be fishers of men.

But how did Jesus get them to this point? What did he do to them to get them to surrender their agendas? How did he prepare them for what was to come? When we really stop to consider this, we soon discover that the answer to this question is quite peculiar. The disciples of Jesus would within three years become the founders of the early church, and the early church would become the foundation for two millennia (and counting) of Christian faith. Multitudes would one day devote their lives to the teaching of these twelve men, and much of what they taught would eventually be inscripturated, called the Word of the living God, and become the canon–or measuring rod–for the faith and practice of Christians at all times and in all places.

It is clear to us looking back that much depended upon these three short years Jesus spent with these untested men—men that he (quite literally) chose off of the street without so much as a conversation.

If I were Jesus, I would have adopted a much longer interview process with multiple layers of assessments. I would have taken pains to ensure that the men I chose were the right men, and that they possessed the right skill sets, emotional sensitivities, and spiritual proclivities to bear the weight of establishing the foundations of the Christian faith. And if I were Jesus, knowing that the preaching of these men would one day become the most important proclamation in the world, I would have spent that three years honing their preaching, fine-tuning their theology, shaping their pedagogy, and crafting a set of learning outcomes that would be foundational for their future ministries in the early church.

But Jesus seems to be concerned about none of these things. In fact, as we read through the gospels with these learning goals in mind, we are struck by the sheer absence of any type of practical instruction provided by Jesus for his disciples. He never teaches them a theology lesson, or gives them any teaching tips. He never warns them about the kinds of problems that they are going to have to face once they embark on the journey of establishing the early church and expanding the mission to reach the world.

What is stranger still is that we almost never see Jesus even calling his disciples to pray. When Jesus prays, he prays alone. Sometimes the disciples are there to watch him pray, but quite frequently he leaves them in order to seek the face of his Father alone. That's baffling to me! If I were Jesus, I would have required my disciples to be up praying every morning at 6 am. But Jesus–as far as the testimonies of the four gospels are concerned–makes no such requirement of his disciples.

Instead, we find Jesus teaching them about the kingdom of God. He begins by spinning out a series of parables in the presence of the multitudes. Then he takes his disciples into the inner room and explains the parables to them. That's all he does with them . . . he teaches them what the kingdom of God is like, and then he demonstrates the power of that kingdom by healing the sick, raising the dead, cleansing the lepers, and casting out demons in their presence. He tells them about the kingdom, and then he shows them the power of the kingdom. And all the disciples do for a while is listen and watch; that is the substance of their discipleship.

The closest Jesus came to providing practical instruction for his disciples was in allowing them to participate in a limited number of miracles. The first was the feeding of the five thousand, at which Jesus blessed the bread and fish, broke them, and then gave them to his disciples with the instruction to feed the people. As the disciples set out in obedience to this command, the miracle took place within their own hands, and the miracle didn't stop until the people were fully fed and twelve baskets of the remainder were collected.

Then he sent them out two by two on a supernatural expedition to heal, deliver, and declare his coming. When they returned, rejoicing that even the demons were subject to them in his name, he instructed them not to marvel at their authority in him, but to marvel that their names were written in the book of life. Even in this situation, Jesus did not actually teach them how to heal; he simply informed them that he had given them the power to do so and then sent them forth to act with that power.

The process by which Jesus engaged his disciples had three basic components: teaching them while they listened, showing them while they watched, and sending them out. And Jesus was so confident in the power of this simple process that he was willing to rest the full weight of God's intended future upon his ability to prepare these twelve ordinary men for their work: the work that would one day bring about such a dramatic, seismic shift in the history of humankind that 2000 later we cannot imagine what the world would be like had the disciples failed in their endeavors.

THE MISSING PIECE

There's another piece to the puzzle that is not readily apparent at first glance. Jesus did nothing more than teach, demonstrate to, and send his disciples; this is true. But when we examine what Jesus taught and why he taught it, we can see why he did not focus on the practical. Jesus knew that if he had focused on the practical he would have perhaps raised up a group of twelve men who knew how to engage in a series of Christian activities. But that is not the same thing as raising up twelve Christians.

This is a point that is very easy for us to miss because we live in a world where Christianity has been confused with Christian activities. A Christian is someone who goes to church, gives her tithes, reads the Bible, spends time in prayer, has good morals and abstains from certain activities deemed sinful by Scripture. If you were to ask the average Christian the difference between engaging in Christian activities and being a mature believer in Jesus Christ, he would have a difficult time answering that question. And in fact, we have come to the point where we equate mature Christianity with mature participation in Christian activities. But Christian maturity and consistent Christian activities are not one and the same reality. It is possible to do all the typical Christian activities, yet remain virtually unchanged in the depths of your heart in relation to God.

Jesus was not interested in raising up twelve religious conformists, so he never required them to pray. Instead, he prayed in their presence with such intimacy, power, and authority that the disciples began to crave this component of his lifestyle. He continued to do this until the day they assembled themselves before him at the close of his prayer time with one earnest request: *Teach us to pray as John also taught his disciples* (Luke 11:1).

Jesus didn't command his disciples to pray; his disciples begged him to teach them how to do it. Prayer was not an activity that Jesus pushed on his disciples; it was a component of his way of life that they longed to learn from him. That way of doing discipleship is far different than the way we do it today!

By praying in the presence of his disciples without requiring his disciples to pray, Jesus successfully communicated the value of prayer to them, and once they had embraced that value, they came and asked him to teach them how to do it. This moment in the ministry of Jesus provides us with the key to understanding his entire process of discipleship. It is this process of discipleship we must discover in order not only to recover the pastoral task, but to fulfill the great commission to make disciples of all nations.

Jesus was not so interested in imparting to his disciples the knowledge of how to perform a series of Christian tasks. The primary concern of Jesus was to impart to his disciples the system of values that undergirded all he did and all he said (as well as all that he did not do or say). Jesus knew that if he told his disciples what to do without imparting the understanding of why they were to do it, they would comply with his religious instructions without contending for his eternal kingdom. But if they were to catch his values and embrace them from the very depths of their hearts, there would be no way to stop them from fulfilling his commission and committing that commission to the next generation as effectively as he committed it to them.

Jesus did not teach tasks, he taught values. All of his teachings were about articulating his values. His primary subject was the Father and his kingdom, and while his teaching embodied the truth of who the Father is and what his kingdom is like, it was also laced with the values of that kingdom. In articulating the values of the kingdom, Jesus taught his disciples not just what the kingdom was like, but how to enter into it and live fully within it. The values that Jesus communicated to his disciples became the roadmap for living life to the full in the knowledge of the Father.

Following Jesus with all of our hearts is not so much about engaging in Christian activities, but about fully embracing the values of Christ so that our hearts beat as his heart beats. This is difficult because our own values do not die easily. The whole process of sanctification is a progressive conflict of values. At every point in our lives, the Holy Spirit causes the values of Jesus to come into conflict with our personal values. If we cling to our own values, our spiritual growth is stunted and we remain as we are. But if we forsake our own way, if we turn to God and are converted, then we will be able to embrace the values of Jesus . . . values that may seem simple and insignificant, but have the power to equip us to turn the world upside down in the 21st century as the apostles did it in the first.

Jesus' values-based model of discipleship teaches us that at the center of the pastoral task is the art of winning the hearts and capturing the imaginations of the people we serve. The disciples of Jesus were mesmerized by the power of his lifestyle, and this is why their hearts were continually open to receive the content of his words. The power of the pastoral task lies not in the words but in the lifestyle of the shepherd. My words will have little to no effect upon people until the character of my spiritual life causes them to marvel at the grace and power of God.

THE STRATEGY OF JESUS

Teach us to pray . . . Once the disciples asked Jesus to teach them to pray, he was free to instruct them without the risk of their prayer being motivated by mere religious conformity. At that point their hearts desired to emulate the lifestyle of Jesus, and this was the first sign that they had made progress on the pathway to maturity in him.

It is at this point that I would expect Jesus to give them some very practical instructions for the cultivation of an ever-deepening communion with the Father. Perhaps he would now tell them what time they should get up in the morning, in what position they should posture themselves when they pray . . . whether to lift their hands or clasp them, whether to bow or kneel. But Jesus taught no such things. Instead, he responded to their ardent cry for instruction by providing them with a children's prayer.

So He said to them, When you pray, say:
Our Father in heaven,
Hallowed be Your name.
Your kingdom come.
Your will be done
On earth as it is in heaven.
Give us day by day our daily bread.
And forgive us our sins,
For we also forgive everyone who is indebted to us.
And do not lead us into temptation,
But deliver us from the evil one. (Luke 11:2–4)

Most of us age out of this prayer by the time we hit ten

years old; the prayer has become somewhat of a nursery rhyme for the modern believer. But it is time for us to rescue this prayer from the sandbox. This prayer is no children's prayer; this prayer has hair on its chest!

We can begin to understand the meaning and significance of the Lord's Prayer once we come to the realization that recitation is not the primary purpose of the prayer. In giving this prayer to his disciples, Jesus was not simply instructing them to recite it every night at bed time. Reciting this prayer once a day, or even multiple times a day, will not by itself result in the cultivation of the kind of prayer life that Jesus exemplified.

We must remember that when the disciples asked Jesus to teach them to pray, implicit in their request was the desire to emulate their rabbi. The cry of their hearts was not just *teach us to pray*; the true cry of their hearts was *teach us to pray like you!* And none of us would ever surmise that all Jesus did all night long on the mountaintop with the Father was recite the Lord's Prayer!

The meaning of the Lord's Prayer opens up to us when we perceive it as the hierarchical articulation of the value system of Jesus. In giving the Lord's Prayer to his disciples, Jesus provided them with a perfect outline of his values. The point was that if the disciples embraced these values in their proper order, they would invariably find themselves praying the way Jesus prayed.

So he begins the prayer with *Our Father*. It is as if he is saying, *I pray the way I pray because I value the Father as my highest value. It is my value for the Father that calls me to the mountaintop and keeps me there all night long.*

In heaven: Jesus not only values the Father, but he values his dwelling place in heaven. We too must value this, and keep our minds on things above (Colossians 3:1).

Then he values the holiness of his Father's name, the coming of his kingdom, the fulfillment of his will, the conformity of earth with heaven, the provision of daily bread, the forgiveness of sins, divine direction and divine deliverance. It is as if he were saying, *These are my values, and if you value the things that I value, you will pray the way I pray.*

The pastoral strategy of Jesus was first to captivate the hearts of his disciples with a compelling vision of a new way of life, and then to provide them with a roadmap for cultivating it. This is the key for understanding the process of shepherding the soul from beginning to end. In all of our dealings with the mind, heart, and the will . . . in all of our discernment of opportune moments for authoritative encouragement, the goal is not merely to promote participation in Christian activities, but to cultivate the values of Jesus.

The realm of the Spirit is the realm in which the values of Jesus are exemplified in their fullness, and this is the true definition of the abundant life that Jesus said he came to bring us. And this explains why the carnal mind is God's enemy. The carnal mind, or the mind of the flesh, simply does not value the things Jesus values. The mind of the flesh does not value the Father, heaven, the holiness of the Father's name, the coming of his kingdom, or the fulfillment of his will . . . In fact, the carnal mind opposes all of the values of Jesus.

The goal of Jesus' discipleship program was not to ensure that his disciples could quote a certain number of Scriptures, or demonstrate proficiency in a particular set of Christian activities. The core objective of Jesus was to teach his disciples to walk fully in the life of the Spirit and to teach others to do the same.

Conclusion

The soul of the shepherd & the Shepherd of souls

In order to effectively shepherd the souls of others, the soul of the shepherd must submit to the Shepherd of souls. While it is popular to assume that we can submit directly to Christ without submitting to anyone else, the fact remains that the true sign we have reverence for Christ is that we submit to one another. Until you have learned how to submit to others, you will never learn how to effectively lead, and until you have learned to allow your soul to be shepherded, you will never learn to effectively shepherd the souls of others.

At the end of the day, your soul can only be shepherded if you submit it to your leaders, and this requires the suspension of judgment and the relinquishment of criticism. Once you have become critical of your leader, your heart begins to build up a resistance to his or her words and your soul begins to drift unchecked into the realm of the flesh. Judgment and criticism are like shields which guard the soul against the word of the Lord by belittling his servants. This can happen so suddenly and so subtly that you won't even realize what has befallen you until you return to your senses.

I personally experienced this back in 2000 as a seminary

student who had learned just enough to be ignorant. I was in the midst of my intensive Greek quarter and was elated by the fact that I was doing so well in the course. For some reason Greek just made sense to me, and I was excelling to the extent that the professor began giving me accolades in front of the class. All the while, I was unaware of the pride growing in my heart—and how it was affecting my intimacy with God.

The wake-up call came one Sunday when I attended a very well-known church in the SoCal area and heard a powerful message being preached. I was tremendously blessed by the message until the preacher quoted Matthew 6:29 and said that Jesus used an imperative in the Greek to exhort his disciples not to worry. When he said that I had this thought: "There is no imperative in the text; it's a prohibitory subjunctive!" And from that moment on I couldn't get anything else out of the sermon because I was distracted by the preacher's incorrect parsing of one Greek phrase!

At the moment I just thought the preacher should have known better, seeing that he had a Ph.D. and many years of preaching experience. But within a few hours it dawned on me that I was being ridiculous. Here was this man, delivering words that were coming as spirit and life, but I couldn't receive them because he had incorrectly described a Greek verb! In that moment my academic knowledge had become a shield that prevented me from receiving the things of the Spirit of God. My pride and criticism had led me to operate with the carnal mind.

Judgment and criticism are born in your heart the moment you feel like you know better than your leaders or that you have uncovered their weaknesses. And this is not only true of your leaders, but of believers in general. Identifying the weaknesses of another believer is one thing; knowing that believer by her weaknesses is another. Identification is a type of discernment, but once the discernment of the weakness of another causes me to *know* him according to that weakness, I have begun judging him (in the sense prohibited by Christ) rather than merely exercising discernment.

Jesus is indeed the Good Shepherd, and he has laid down his life for the sheep. He is the Shepherd and Overseer of our souls, and we must direct our souls to return to him each and every day. He is leading his flock like a shepherd, and he is leading us to streams of living water. But he has determined to shepherd our souls through our interactions with one another, and to demonstrate his love for us as we pour out our love for one another.

As we engage the world of the 21st century, the power of our witness will largely be determined by the state of our engagement with the pastoral task. We can only impact the world evangelistically if we are first able to engage the church pastorally. If we succeed evangelistically and fail pastorally, we will bring people out of the world but not into the church, and this is perhaps the explanation of why the vast majority of new converts in churches across denominations are no longer walking with Christ less than one year after making a confession of faith.

God is looking for shepherds . . . not necessarily vocational pastors, but men and women who are willing to embrace the heart of the Good Shepherd. In order to embrace this heart, we must reject the popular disdain for the pastoral that has plagued our contemporary Christian world.

We have witnessed an explosive reemphasis upon the apostolic and prophetic offices in the past century, and this is a wonderful thing. But in the process we have somehow found it necessary to relegate the pastoral office to a place of inferiority compared with these exalted positions. In doing so, we have forgotten that even though Jesus is once spoken of as the apostle and high priest of our confession (Hebrews 3:1), he does not identify himself as the good apostle, or the good prophet. Instead he identifies himself as the Good Shepherd . . . the good pastor! (John 10:11, 14)

Once more God is waiting for the offering of Abel, the offering of the shepherd, and it is the only offering that he will look upon with favor. If your heart is ready to embrace the heart of the Good Shepherd, his heart is ready to receive your offering as an offering in righteousness.

Now may the God of peace who brought up our Lord Jesus from the dead, that great Shepherd of the sheep, through the blood of the everlasting covenant, make you complete in every good work to do his will, working in you what is well pleasing in his sight, through Jesus Christ, to whom be glory forever and ever. Amen. (Hebrews 13:20-21)

Notes

[1] The image of being "slain in the flesh" is a play on the image of being "slain in the Spirit." Just as one is physically overpowered by the Spirit in the experience of being slain in the Spirit, so we can describe the experience of being overpowered by temptation as being slain in the flesh.

[2] At the same time there continue to be a host of reputable biblical scholars who continue to support Mosaic authorship of the Pentateuch. Among them are William Henry Green, author of *Unity of the Book of Genesis* (1895) and Duane Garrett, author of *Rethinking Genesis: The Sources and Authorship of the First Book of the Bible* (2000).

[3] This does not preclude the possibility that Moses used source materials that were available to him. Whether he used sources or not, the impetus of the writing of the text was the inspiration of the Holy Spirit, rather than a mere editorial process.

[4] Yes, that was indeed a quotation from Eminem's "Lose Yourself."

[5] Augustine, The *Confessions of St Augustine* (London: Griffith Farran Browne & Co Limited, 1886), p. 1.

[6] Paschal, *Pensées* (New York; Penguin Books, 1966), p. 75.

Made in the USA
Middletown, DE
02 July 2021

43511291R00091